Ash "Bash" Perrin is the founder and CEO of The Flying Seagull Project, a UK-based charity that brings happiness to children around the world.

The Flying Seagull Project is a troupe of entertainers who engage children and adults in games, art, music, craft, circus skills and performances. They have worked in a wide range of settings, from children's hospitals, orphanages and refugee camps to schools, festivals and parties. The Flying Seagull philosophy is that everyone – man, woman and child – has the right to put aside the cares of life and smile for a while.

The Real Play Revolution is Ash Perrin's first book.

Why we need to be silly
with our kids – and how to do it

THE REAL PLAY
REVOLUTION

Ash
Perrin

WATKINS
Sharing Wisdom Since 1893

The Real Play Revolution
Ash Perrin

This edition first published in the UK and USA in 2019 by
Watkins, an imprint of Watkins Media Limited
Unit 11, Shepperton House
89–93 Shepperton Road
London
N1 3DF

enquiries@watkinspublishing.com

Design and typography copyright © Watkins Media Limited 2019

Text copyright © Ash Perrin
Illustrations copyright © Jack Kelly

10 9 8 7 6 5 4 3 2 1

Designed by Georgina Hewitt

Typeset by Integra

Printed and bound in Great Britain by TJ International Ltd, Padstow, Cornwall

A CIP record for this book is available from the British Library

ISBN: 978-1-786782-23-6

www.watkinspublishing.com

To Master Joey Coconut, for being your full self, making us laugh until our bellies hurt, and for reminding us it doesn't have to make sense to be funny!

CONTENTS

INTRODUCTION

What is play? How do we do it? And why does it matter?

My name is Ash Perrin, although I'm also known as Bash the clown. I am a professional noise-maker, childhood conservationist, rabble-rouser and life-long play enthusiast. I have spent over 15 years working with children in every corner of the globe, from the billionaires of London and Dubai, to children living on the streets of Ghana and Cambodia. With my devoted and wonderful team who make up The Flying Seagull Project, we have shown love through laughter and play in orphanages, hospitals, refugee camps, conflict zones, homes for the elderly (yes, they like to play too) and just about everywhere in between!

WHO ARE THE FLYING SEAGULLS?

I had been working for a while in various forms of performance art, play work, entertainment and leading workshops when, in 2008, the moment came for me to pull it all together by creating The Flying Seagull Project. The name was inspired by Richard Bach's book *Jonathan Livingston Seagull*. The main message of that book became the founding principle of my work: that there are no limits other than those we put on ourselves, and that everyone has the incredible potential to be happy and feel confident.

For over a decade, I have led this amazing team of clowns, dancers, puppet makers, circus artists and energizers across four continents in 23 countries, sharing play with more than 115,000 children, and now I want to try to share with you some stuff we've figured out along the way. With The Flying Seagull Project, I've played Bulldog with society's forgotten communities, as well as Pirates at the UK's biggest festivals. I've worked one to one with kids with behavioural challenges in England, and led circus sessions with more than 800 children at once in rural Ghana. I once even ran a play week in the Amazon rainforest! I tell you all of this just so you will believe me when I say I've thought about this a lot – and the one thing I am now more sure of than ever, is that there is an urgent need for play in all areas of society.

I'm talking about Real Play, where voices are loud, and eyes sparkle, and imaginations soar, and laughter is in abundance.

WHY IS PLAY IMPORTANT?

During the course of my work with The Flying Seagull Project, I have come across many individuals around the world who feel disempowered, disenfranchised and down-right unhappy – and far too many of these have been children. While there are many reasons for their distress, including societal position, disability, religious intolerance, poverty and war forcing them to flee their homelands, the linking factor for all of them is their resulting sense of not being good enough and not belonging.

This is why The Flying Seagull Project aims to combat these situations by creating childhood experiences, games sessions, creative workshops and cultural happenings that allow the children to connect with their innate right to feel good, whoever they are and wherever they are.

We have been blessed to learn a craft that is in danger of slipping from mainstream society and have seen first-hand its ability to return energy, confidence and mile-wide smiles to kids' faces. That craft is play, Real Play, and in this book I hope to explore what that really means, figure out the best way to deliver it, and once and for all establish it as an essential part of everyone's life.

HOW DOES THIS BOOK WORK?

Whether you are a parent, teacher, play worker or any sort of professional working with children, I will be offering you practical guidance, top tips and real-life evidence that shows just how important play is for all of us. We will be looking at the art and philosophy of play and at how to play well.

In Chapter 1, "Laugh Like Your Life Depends on It (It Does!)", I'll be touching upon the science of play and why it is so important for us mentally and physically, with games to get everyone in the mood for some serious silliness. Chapter 2, "Play Properly!" explains the basic principles of how to play with heart and soul, and what it is we're really offering to kids in play. In Chapter 3, "Let Go", we'll be looking at shedding our own inhibitions and hang-ups, before going on to ramp up the energy in Chapter 4, "Get Energized". Chapter 5, "Be Brave and Go Big" is about gaining the confidence that enables us to let that energy explode, knowing we can down-turn the volume when we need to. In Chapter 6, "Creativity Needs You!", the focus is on creativity, what this really means and how to shepherd kids through those crisis moments that often precede imaginative breakthroughs. Next, in Chapter 7, "Meet Challenge with Positivity", we'll be tackling ways to meet challenges with optimism. While Chapter 8, "Start Your Own Real Play Revolution", brings it all together to set you on the path to doing just that!

TOOLS FOR REAL PLAY

Throughout this book you'll find plenty of game plans and activity suggestions to help establish an optimistic and positive rapport with kids, whether in the classroom, after school or at home with the family. There's a mixture of traditional games, some of which you might recognize, as well as brand-new games and unique activities invented by me and the team at The Flying Seagull Project. Toward the end of each chapter, you'll find a lucky dip of extra group games for you to enjoy. While most of the games are suitable for kids at primary school level, I have purposefully not listed suggested age ratings for these activities, so that you are free to use your own judgement and adapt them according to who is playing.

As far as basic kit goes, as a troupe of professional clowns, The Flying Seagull Project is lucky to have lots of resources to hand, but here are the only essentials you need:

- a sense of humour
- low-to-no sense of shame
- imagination
- and lots of enthusiasm and energy!

Music can also help to create a playful environment. For extra energy, play fast music during speedy activities, gentle music for quieter activities, "suspicious" music for games like Wink Murder (see page 48), manic music for One Minute Madness (see page 81) and upbeat music to get the room feeling positive at the start. If you have the skill to play an instrument and make live music then that is even better!

A few other pieces of improvised kit (e.g. from thrift stores/charity shops or raiding the wardrobe) are optional extras. With encouragement, and your example, most kids will only need a bit of imagination to enjoy a game.

PLAN AHEAD

Whatever game or games you are going to play, I recommend planning ahead (see Chapter 2). And I also recommend you have at least twice as many activities as you think you are going to need. I call this "double plan", by which I mean you have double the amount that you think you'll ever get through. This allows you to be flexible, change your mind on the spot if necessary and never get to a point where you feel like you're buying time. Whatever you're planning, double it, and then at the very least you can do everything twice as fast and still not run out of activities.

If you feel that the kids are getting bored, then the activity has gone on for too long and it's time to change the game. If you find you are dragging out every game, or "milking it" as we call it, then you have not planned your play session properly, and you are probably guilty of "plamming" (play-scamming). This is when you're planning ways to kill the time rather than fill the time!

Plan, don't plam! (This is mainly targeted at those of you who work with kids, rather than at home, but I think if we're all honest there's a bit of plamming at home too sometimes!)

Games are not something to fill space or time with; rather, they're about setting that space alight and creating energy that's fun to be around.

PLAY FOR THE FUTURE

The intrusion of screens into playtime, and the validity of gaming as a play resource rather than an entertainment medium, has created an interesting time in our world. Never have we been more connected and able to communicate with so many people around the world, yet never have loneliness and social anxiety been so prevalent in our lives. To find the root of this sense of alienation, and hopefully move through these challenges, remembering the strengths of a more traditional play landscape and recognizing what it was that we once experienced within it, is a good way to start.

Play cannot be owned, it needs no money, and it requires no master's degree. It just needs you, kids – and a big bag full of glowing, loving, positive ENERGY. The opportunity to share good times and be happy together lies in our hands.

In this book, I propose that we stand up, open our arms and embrace it, before it is lost forever ...

CHAPTER 1

LAUGH LIKE YOUR LIFE DEPENDS ON IT (IT DOES!)

"A good laugh heals a lot of hurts."

Play shapes us as human beings. Yet, as we get older, it can be tempting to write off play as something flippant that we either ought to leave behind us in childhood, or turn into a deadly serious business instead. In the world of work, for instance, play often becomes linked to competitiveness and to winning, rather than to growth and happiness: "he's back in the game", "she's a key player", "they smashed it out of the park" – you get the idea! The danger is that if we simply write off play as irreverent and superfluous, or as something that entails hard graft and competition, we are potentially dismissing the first decade of development that takes place in our lives.

Nearly everything that forms the foundation of who we are and how we understand and interact with the world is based in childhood play and experimentation. The very first gurgles and burbles that a baby makes are playful copies of sounds they've heard. In the same way, if you watch a baby learn to walk, it looks at first like the baby is trying out a new game rather than mastering a life skill. If it wasn't, the potential dangers involved in, for example, learning how to stand upright would probably impede their progress or leave a negative impact on them in the long term. Play is how children research and learn about the world in order to equip themselves with the tools needed for life. The joy of play provides a safety net for learning.

Over the years, I've been lucky enough to work with many influential people and practitioners within the world of play, such as the highly acclaimed Professor Deborah Youdell. I first met Deborah while performing at a festival in the UK, where she and her daughter were having lots of fun with some of the activities that I'll be sharing in this book. Afterwards, Deborah asked me about my pedagogical background and the influences on my approach to play. Now I can hold my own in a conversation or mild debate, but I have to tell you that at that time I had no idea who my pedagogical influences were and I certainly wasn't aware of any formal techniques underpinning my work. I just knew that whatever I was doing was working, and helping to spread a bit of happiness and laughter.

Deborah stayed in touch after the show and shared some incredibly interesting and inspiring pieces of work with me written by such practitioners as Paolo Freire from Brazil. She then came to more of our performances and asked if I would be interested in a collaborative research project. I mention this not in order to exaggerate the importance of academic research or to place a higher value on it in relation to lived experience, but rather to show how both academia and an experiential understanding of play are entirely in agreement: play achieves and means much more than just something kids do to kill time in the garden. Even though I quite obviously believe in the benefits of play and having a good time, there's nothing wrong with taking on board a little bit of research to bring home just how important laughter really is. So, ladies and gentlemen, may I present you with some science.

SOME SCIENCE

The following extract is taken from "The Flying Seagull Project – Joining the Laugh-olution", a paper written by Professor Deborah Youdell for the Public Service Academy, University of Birmingham. In it, she draws on the work of Flying Seagull and looks at compelling evidence from the social sciences, neuroscience and biochemistry about the importance of laughter and collective physical play for building social bonds, resolving conflict, creating cohesive communities, developing resilience and securing personal and social well-being. She notes:

> Our intuition and experience tell us that laughing is a good thing, and social research confirms the role that laughter plays in creating and sustaining social bonds as well as social boundaries and in making us feel good.
>
> Neuroscience identifies two distinct types of laughter: voluntary laughter which plays an important part in communication, and involuntary laughter which is a more primitive part of social interaction shared by many mammals and is important for creating and maintaining social bonds, regulating feelings, and making us feel better. The brain responds differently to these two forms of laughter and works hard to process the potential meaning of laughter – a skill developed during childhood and early adulthood (Scott 2013).*
>
> The release of endorphins during laughter contributes to the bonding effect of shared laughter. Endorphins are neuropeptides – opioids thought of popularly as "happy" or "feel good" hormones – that have a role in

the management of pain and in building and maintaining relationships. Endorphins are released during gentle stroking, laughter and group participation in music, singing, dancing and playing games or sport. The social aspects of these activities are important to the levels of endorphin activation; indeed, synchronized activities see a large increase in endorphin activation. The physical exhaustion caused by emptying lungs and the exhaustion of abdominal muscles that results from involuntary laughter also contribute to endorphin release (Dunbar 2012).**

In psychoanalysis the idea of jouisance suggests the possibility of re-experiencing the joy that we experienced as infants before we understood ourselves and the rules and troubles of the social world. The uncontrollable belly laugh or the moment of forgetting ourselves as we are caught up in play can be seen as ways of reconnecting with this joy.

It is clear, then, that vitality, joy and laughter experienced in the present have beneficial effects that persist well into the future. They make important contributions to our capacity to make and maintain bonds, to develop sustained relationships, relieve stress and resolve conflict, and to social cohesion more widely. They are a significant part of our neural networks and the biochemistry of our brains. In short, they are essential ingredients of personal, community and societal well-being. Where funders and policy makers are concerned to invest scarce resources in activities that will have significant benefits in the future, investing in laughter makes sense.

According to the science, it seems it's laughter – not money – that really makes the world go round.

LAUGHTER IS THE BEST MEDICINE

There have been many moments over the years that have stood out for me, where laughter has broken every rule and astonished me with its impact. One particular instance took place in a hospital in Albania, where The Flying Seagull Project was collaborating with our friends in the Humanitas Charity on a project called Health and Happiness. As part of their work, Humanitas have a dynamic medical team who care for people living in poverty and crisis situations, while training the local staff to deliver treatments more effectively. Our "laughter is the best medicine" team deliver pre- and post-operative clown support for kids facing surgery or coping with chronic illness, and in this instance they were working alongside Humanitas as they screened children for hydrocephalus.

For a lot of the kids, it was their first time in hospital, and for all of them it was scary. That's where our team came in, using all the elements of play to inspire laughter and confidence and turn the whole experience into a positive one. The result that day was mind blowing. Within moments the children were laughing and playing in the doctor's room; in fact, when it was time for them to go home, some were actually sad to leave, saying they couldn't wait to come back to hospital.

I have a huge amount of respect for medical professionals, and though I know why hospitals are scary, in some ways it's a real shame. It's amazing that ultra-talented doctors and surgeons can repair hearts and fix spines, and that their work can improve a child's life forever. With the simple addition of laughter, the trio of needs is complete: Health, Happiness and Hope.

So, now we've looked at how play shapes our development and can help healing, it's time to put the theory into practice. Let's get going with some activities so we can experience the power of play for ourselves.

THE INCREDIBLE POWER OF PLAY

Playing and laughing together is one of the most therapeutic, exciting, connecting and loving experiences we can hope for. When we laugh, all the things that have been bothering us or pulling us apart disappear, and just because of a wide-mouth, toothy grin everything's okay again – at least in the ways that matter. Yet sometimes the last thing we want to do when we get home is laugh. Working all hours of the day, worrying about finding the money for the rent or the mortgage, trying to keep the house running and giving the children what we think they need for a happy, stable and well-adjusted childhood, it can be near impossible to find the energy and the peace of heart and mind we need to come home and join in the fun that's waiting for us behind the front door.

There is so much pressure to "provide" for children, but actually what children need to have a happy, stable and well-adjusted life is not all the things that they see on TV or that the neighbours may have. What they need is YOU. You encouraging them and teaching them and loving them and holding them through the challenges that childhood presents. What we remember from our childhood is not the size of the house we grew up in, or the decent double-glazing, or the well-balanced, nutritious diet we were fed. What we remember are the experiences we have with those who care for us. And that's not just our immediate parents or guardians, but also our family friends, neighbours, teachers, football coaches and so on. We remember the people who believed in us or took time out to make us feel special. For me, it's the funny stuff I remember most – my godfather Jeff pretending that his legs were tied in a knot and that he couldn't get up, or my mum and dad's Black Magic dance routine, whispering down a walking stick. These are the moments that shape you; it's the comedy and the playfulness that make you see that life can be fun as well as serious and tough.

KIDS' COMEDY CORNER

And all this is why we need Kids' Comedy Corner! The idea was born during a rainy afternoon at the Green Man Festival. It was pouring with rain and the stage was surrounded by wide-eyed if somewhat damp kids eager to be entertained. Something special was needed … a flash of inspiration, a dodgy New York accent, an old-fashioned microphone, a pile of costume jackets and hats and BAM! something special was born: Kids' Comedy Corner! Everyone there, kids, parents and performers, knew immediately we had stumbled over a winning formula. KCC has since grown to minor legend status, a festival must.

Regardless of the advancements in digital technology and computer gaming and whatever else has changed for children today, there are some things that remain enshrined in truth. One of these is that a kid telling a joke, however badly delivered it may be, is still the cutest, funniest, most heart-warming thing you'll ever see. Most kids don't hold back when they see an opportunity to show their adults just how much personality they have. They will plough enthusiastically into a joke without having any idea how to finish it. Every child has a favourite joke that makes them absolutely belly laugh every time they tell it, and the opportunity to tell it is too much to resist. All we do with Kids' Comedy Corner is create an opportunity for the kids to tell their joke. And if any are a little shy and embarrassed, we give them fancy-dress costumes and a New York accent (or as close to one as they can manage) to hide behind while they do it.

Some jokes are actually genuinely funny, some kids are just so hilarious you'd laugh if they said the periodic table and others are just so utterly and totally useless at joke telling that they are the funniest of all, with everyone in stitches at just how outrageously wrong and muddled it is. The wonderful thing about Kids' Comedy Corner is not to tell great jokes, but just to connect with your kids and with each other by telling any jokes we have. Really it's just an excuse to celebrate personality and humour. A catchphrase that we say during the game is "it don't have to make sense to be funny" – and that is absolutely the truth. Nothing has to make sense to be funny.

Here's an adaptation of Kids' Comedy Corner to bring back some of that play and laughter and remind you why you come home in the first place. Depending on where you are, it could be called Family Comedy Corner, Holiday Comedy Corner, School Comedy Corner ... you can preface it with whatever you like, but the concept remains the same. It's all about connecting and uniting through shared humour, comedy and laughter.

Don't spend a lot of money buying props. You probably have a tatty old sheet about the place and it's amazing what you can find in a thrift store/charity shop for minimal outlay. Letting your kids raid your wardrobe for funny over-sized garments is also an option.

You will need:
Old, plain bedsheet
Pens (to write on fabric and card)
White card for prompt signs and microphone cut-out
Thrift store/charity shop clothes for costumes
Music
Everyone's favourite food
Your phone and charger plus a flat surface or (if you have one) a tripod, for support.

You don't need:
TV
Facebook, Instagram, etc.
Emails
To be late

Step 1. Invite the guests: once a month, on a Friday, everybody in the family gets to invite two or three of their best friends over. For the parents, this doesn't necessarily mean your son's best friend's parents, but your actual friends! People you would genuinely choose to spend Friday night with.

Step 2. Find some costumes: go down to your local thrift store/ charity shop and buy some potentially comic clothes, such as blazers, trilby hats, ugly ties. Get some glasses and pop the lenses out. See if you can create a real mad box of clothing that might be worn in a comedy club. Choose clothes that are as ill-fitting and silly-looking as you can and chuck them all in a box. If they fit well and make you look gorgeous, they're the wrong ones.

Step 3. Make the props: you will need a nice, old-fashioned microphone. You can draw a simple outline on a piece of white card and cut it out. Or use a toy microphone, if you have one.

If I were you, I would also make prompt signs as if for a live show:

OH YEAH?
WHO'S THERE?
LOUDER!
APPLAUSE
GO WILD!

And so on. If there's a knock-knock joke, hold up the "who's there?" sign as fast as you can. It's great fun to take turns holding up the signs and even more funny when you get in a muddle trying to find the right one.

Step 4. Choose the music: it's fun to play some music for performers walking off and on. I normally play some Tom Waits or some kind of saxophone jazz. Maybe Mum can choose one week, and Uncle John another. Or maybe take it in turns, so that each performer has their own special piece of music, like a boxer coming into the ring!

Step 5. Get in some treats: get in the food you like – pizza, takeaway curry, popcorn by the lorry load, whatever you want to eat. Allow the feeling of a celebration to sneak in, as that's what this is. A celebration of the outrageous good fortune you all have to be in each other's life!

Step 6. Set the scene: take the television out of the room. I don't mean cover it up, I mean take it out of the room completely, and where the television goes – which is probably the focal point design-wise of the room – hang a bespoke decorated bed sheet. That sheet is designed and created by the whole family together, even those that can't draw neatly! Mark out the words "Family Comedy Corner" in big letters. You could write the letters and get the kids to colour them in. Draw some pictures if you like. Do it however you want to do it, but it should be nice and homemade and beautifully imperfect. DO NOT PRINT IT FROM THE COMPUTER! Now hang it up just where the television was.

Step 7. Make it important: when Friday night comes, make sure you get home on time. Tell your office or wherever it is you work that you're leaving on time, whatever happens. Tell them why, and be proud of making it a priority. This night is sacred, a special time when you and your family and friends come together in your front room. If this isn't worth getting away on time for, then I don't know what is!

Step 8. Now have some fun ...: one by one, you take it in turns to swagger up, cool as a cucumber. In that comedy New York drawl you say the following script ...

> Comedian: "My name is ___ and I gotta joke to tell!"
> Audience: "Oh yeah?"
> Comedian: "Yeah and it goes like this ... [then tells joke in New York accent]."

Mums and dads, just for once let yourself be seen and tell your joke. Whatever you do, you are not allowed to not take part. Everybody takes their turn. Watch their faces when you walk up with a funny costume on, talking in a ridiculous accent. Your kids will be wide-eyed, grinning from ear to ear, and what you're doing in that moment is making a memory. You're making a memory of the true you, the real you revealed, the awkward you if you're awkward and the shy you if you're shy. Not everybody's a performer but that doesn't matter: to see you walk up there and try will mean the absolute universe to those kids.

There's no such thing as being too old to tell a joke, and even the teenagers take part. They may fight it at first but, trust me, I've done this for over ten years at festivals – everybody is desperate to take part and the sight of pure joy in the eyes of those watching is worth all the money in the world.

Make a rule that everybody has to take at least five turns. If you warn your guests, you can spend a month before planning your jokes. You don't have to force it to last all night, but make sure it's a good hour and make it special. Don't scrimp, don't cheat, don't take a shortcut and dodge your turn. Take the time to go and buy that bed sheet, really take the TV out of the room. There's nothing worse than the shape of a TV behind the bed sheet ... Play is not a spectator sport so don't spectate, really engage. Don't hold back and put them on the spot: you've got to embarrass yourself to make it an equal evening of sharing a part of yourself and really playing together.

The wonderful thing is you can play this game as many times as you like, as there is a never-ending supply of awful jokes so you can repeat it as often as you want.

Step 9. Capture it on your phone: now here's the treasure for afterwards. Make sure it's all recorded. Don't hold your phone up; put it on a flat surface, a tripod or some other support and leave it to record the whole thing. Put your phone on the charger to make sure the batteries don't run out, check the memory so there's space. I promise you, if you capture this, you are going to have the most golden and priceless piece of film you've ever owned.

The next time that you're driving home from work or you're getting the train, and you've got that feeling of a dark cloud tied to your hat, your shoulders are tensed up, your mind is racing, your brows furrowed and you're feeling like nothing could

cheer you up, stop before you get home. At least 100 metres down the road. Open up that video and watch it; and there you're going to see your boyfriend/wife/daughter/son/mother – whoever it is. You're going to see them grinning, red and embarrassed, telling a funny joke; and if that doesn't make you realize the reason you went to work in the first place, and how incredible the people waiting for you at home are, then nothing will. Leave your boss and the deadline on the train, and arrive home, heart open, with a sparkle in your eye.

If you're at work and you're starting to feel lost, isolated or stressed, take a giggle break. Pop outside and rather than have a cigarette, scroll back to last month's Family Comedy Corner and watch a bit of the good stuff.

Finally I would recommend you don't put any footage on

Facebook or social media sites. Keep this for yourselves. If you like, make it into a DVD so others in the group can share it, but this is your private life as a family. Make it sacred.

I promise you that when you're 70 years old, watching this footage on some sort of futuristic holodeck, there's going to be nothing that melts your heart and lifts your spirits and brings a happy loving tear to your eye than that video footage of your little boy or your little girl age six trying to do a New York accent telling knock-knock jokes that don't make sense.

Enjoy Your Kids

It may be a cliché but it's the people that you share your home with that matter most, rather than the size of the home you live in. In the end, it's about how we spend our time together, not where we spend it. Home is about a sense of belonging, not just bricks and walls.

No matter how serious work and other stressors in life can get – and let's be honest, it can get pretty serious – if we lose track of the reason we get up in the morning and the reason we go out and try to make money or at least earn a living, then there's really no point in doing it anymore. If you lose your golden family moments in the pursuit of a job, only to find that by the time you retire your kids are grown up and gone... then what's the point? Enjoy them – and let them enjoy you right now.

GROWN-UP WRANGLING

Grown-up wrangling is a chance to reverse the tables and put the children in charge. For anyone who has played the board game Hungry Hippos, this is the Wild West, real-life version. This game works best when there are lots of players (the ideal number is

20 children divided into four teams), so it's one to play with friends and neighbours if you need to make up the numbers.

You will need:
Equal numbers of adults to kids
Two to four lightweight "lassos" (e.g. a plastic hula hoop with a rope tied to it or a large fishing net – but no sharp edges or hard surfaces), depending on the number of teams
Space to run about in
Music to play to (optional)
A timer (optional)

To play, separate the kids into teams while the grown-ups form a herd. Each team has a lasso and chooses who is going to go first. When the music starts, or you set the timer (if using) and shout, "Go!", a child from each group will run into the herd of grown-ups

Play It Like You Mean It

I would encourage all grown-ups to play properly, as it's no fun if you allow yourself to be caught or conquered straightaway. There is nothing wrong with a challenge, and it is no bad thing if it is slightly difficult to defeat a grown-up: a) it makes a game worth playing, b) it allows a more authentic exchange between all the players.

and try to capture one of them in the lasso and return them to the pen. The pen is made by the other children in the team holding hands to form a circle.

On the successful capture of a grown-up, the child hands the net to the next team member and swaps places with them to secure the adult in the pen. Then the next child seeks their own grown-up to capture. The game is won when there are no more adults remaining or time has run out.

WORLD'S GREATEST DISASTER MASTER: CHEERING TUMBLES

As anyone who has children or who works with them knows, their sense of self-preservation and personal safety can be slightly underdeveloped. This is something that you have to be aware of as a responsible parent or leader. However, no matter if you're Mary Poppins herself, there will be moments when children lose their balance, trip on shoelaces or take a tumble for seemingly no reason whatsoever.

Now, obviously it's important to assess any injuries swiftly and professionally – and I can't stress that enough. Any incident of any level should be taken seriously and treated as such. However, there is scope for an upbeat response to minor scrapes and low-level injuries. If you're playing on grass and somebody takes a tumble, and is obviously not injured beyond a slight grass stain on the knee and maybe a dented ego, then now's the time to crown your master of disaster.

One of the things we've found over the years at The Flying Seagull Project is that by cheering tumbles and even praising a child in a humorous, over-the-top, Olympic-announcer-style way for their ability to perform stunts – even awarding points from the judges – then when there is only a slight graze or a bit of a bump, it's not that you ignore the fact that they've been hurt, it's more that you facilitate their swift return to the group by flooding the situation with upbeat energy and laughter. I have a large number of rosettes that I award for the best tumbles. Rather than encourage children to perform more dangerous acts, it simply removes some of the potential embarrassment caused by the fall.

Not that embarrassment is necessarily a bad thing; sometimes the ability to laugh at ourselves can be the funniest thing of all and a life skill that will see us through challenging times ahead.

DON'T-LOOK-DOWN SPEED DRAWING

Don't-look-down speed drawing is fun, fast and a great way to connect with people. If, for instance, your kids have been arguing or are in a particularly volatile mood, this can be a quite fun way to take them out of that headspace and push them into an on-the-spot art experience. It requires them to be completely in the moment, and quite often they will then simply forget what they were angry about in the first place.

Likewise, if you are running a session with a group, this exercise can create an unusual and eccentric punctuation point at which to break up the session and change the direction of the energy.

You will need:
Two or more people to partner up (although you can form
groups of three)
Pen and paper

The idea is to draw a non-stop portrait without removing your
pen from the paper. However, the added twist is that you're not
allowed to look down. Keep staring into the face of your partner
and attempt to draw the best picture you can of them without
glancing down at the paper.

There are at least two reasons why this is funny: the first is
because the picture you end up with can sometimes make
Picasso look like a square; the second is the unusually bizarre,
intense stare on your face when you're looking at someone
and concentrating on something else. Either way, you'll end up
with some pretty ludicrous pictures which, when framed on the
wall of your classroom or the stairs of your home, will never fail
to raise a giggle.

A FRIENDLY, FUNNY FACE CAUGHT ON KODAK

The mention of Kodak
film and Polaroid cameras
takes me back to the
1980s, when Polaroid
pioneered the idea of
instant photography:
you clicked a button and
a colour photo popped
out of the camera
straightaway, without the
need for a phone or laptop

to display and print it. In the same way, it's fun to capture a mental snapshot of funny moments.

The method is that when something funny happens that makes people laugh, one of you grabs an imaginary camera, frames the shot and says "click". Then you can mentally archive the image of your good friend, teacher or granny's face laughing.

When you're next feeling overworked, stressed, frustrated, or the kids are struggling, recall that Kodak comedy moment. Picture those happy faces again, picking out all the details and eye sparkles – and remember why they were laughing. Thinking of your loved ones in this way is a fast, warm and lovely way to cheer up a mood and make you laugh again.

GAMES TO GET YOU GIGGLING

When life seems to be getting everyone down, here's a handy toolkit of games to help raise the energy and get everyone laughing again.

GAME 1: TV DUBBING

This game is perfect for a fast laugh and to spice up TV time.

You will need:
A TV
A voice
At least two or three players where possible (though you can play this by yourself too!)

Mute the sound on the TV and take it in turns to do the voices for the characters. Allocate who is who, and mix it up: for instance, Dad being a little girl or Mum voicing a rabbit are both good options for a giggle. The first few attempts will be clumsy at best, but after a while you will get the knack. It's quick, it's silly, and won't fail to find a grin.

GAME 2: TAG-TEAM STARE DOWN

This is a variation on the classic staring competition, but rather than not blinking, it's about not smiling.

You will need:
Four or more players (it must be an even number)
A bell
Two chairs
Room to sit facing each other with someone standing behind
A poker face!

To add extra spice to this game, you have a tag-team partner behind you. The job of the seated person is simply to keep staring and not smile or laugh, while the second team-mate stands behind the seated person and does whatever they like to make the facing seated person crack up – leap around, make crazy noises, pull faces – there are no holds barred. The final twist, though, is that each team has a three-credit tag-out option. They can ring the bell, which freezes the action and the two team-mates swap place. This means if you're about to lose it and grin or giggle you can tag out and buy extra time. Whichever team keeps their poker face for the longest wins.

GAME 3: WONKY WARDROBE CHALLENGE

This is a high-speed, dress-up challenge essentially – but it's wonky because the clothing you put on shouldn't be of the right size, as this just adds to the fun.

You will need:

Two players (or equal teams)

Enough room for the players to fling clothes around (so no ornaments nearby)

A huge pile of clothing (enough for the players to be swamped in clothes) of various sizes, shapes and colours, including tops, bottoms – trousers and skirts, gloves, socks and headgear

A whistle/bell/air horn/starter gun!

Measure out the clothing into equal piles. Next, blow the whistle. At this point, there are two different ways you can play the game:

1. The two players have less than a minute to put on as many items of clothing as possible. The player wearing the most at the end of the allotted time wins that round.
2. The first person to put on all of the clothing in front of them wins.

It doesn't really matter which one of these ways you choose as they're both lots of fun. I recommend having a quick picture-pose session at the end of each round, as the absolute ridiculousness of the final product of the Wonky Wardrobe Challenge is something you probably want to frame and stick on the classroom wall or up in the hallway.

NATURALLY PLAYFUL

The power of Real Play is that everybody can take part – and in fact I believe deep down in my bones that the truest human state is a playful one. From romance to family life, in work and in study, I think one of the most genuine ways of being ourselves is through play, and rather than being something we have to learn, it is more an instinct we need to remember.

Now let's go forth and laugh together ... And that's an order!

*Scott, S. 2013. Why We Laugh, TED Talks, www.ted.com/talks/sophie_scott_why_we_laugh?language=en

**Dunbar, R. I. M., Baron, R., Frangou, A., Pearce, E., van Leeuwen, E. J. C., Stow, J., . . . van Vugt, M. (2012). Social laughter is correlated with an elevated pain threshold. Proceedings of the Royal Society of London B: Biological Sciences, 279(1731), 1161-1167.

CHAPTER 2

PLAY PROPERLY!

**"My mum played and, to my surprise, she let me
lead and called me wise!"**

Playing properly is not necessarily the same thing as playing
"nicely". Playing properly is about being honest, and acknowledging
the strengths and weaknesses of everyone involved. Playing properly
is also about being clear about what it is that we are offering and
having an end goal. It's about getting some serious structure into
our silliness, and keeping in mind the following aspects:

- Who is going to take part?
- What is the end goal: what do you hope to achieve through it?
- How are you going to achieve this?

KEEP IT REAL

When you are thinking about who is going to take part in play,
think first about yourself and any adult participants: who are you?
Are you playful, are you clever, are you sporty, are you very funny,

or are you really kind? If you find your strengths and express them in your work, you will have the most success of all. However, if you try to mimic another person or ignore the essence of who you are, kids will spot you for a fake from a mile away and you will miss out on a major resource: yourself.

So who are you? What are your talents? And where could you still grow as a person?

We should all – adults and children alike – recognize our strong points, and be proud of what we know we can offer. Playing small and not daring to reveal to others a strength we possess benefits no one. On the flip side, the same applies to our less-strong areas: recognizing these too is part of playing properly. I have learned the hard way that we cannot do everything by ourselves, and knowing what we're less good at can actually be liberating and ultimately empowering, as it gives us insight into others' strengths and encourages us to work as part of a team – with all separate parts creating a whole. Also, if we keep on hiding the weak bits of ourselves, we won't move past them. So identify your weaknesses and be as proud of these as of all the other elements that make you who you are.

It's important that we adults allow kids to see our imperfections and shortcomings at times. Every child will struggle at some point and watch friends or peers excel where they stumble. Witnessing a confident and warm parent figure or role model fail without self-judgement allows them to see that failure is not a problem. (For more on becoming a role model, see Chapter 8.)

While teaching unicycle in Romania, I was simultaneously learning it. When Robert, a young man aged 12, quickly surpassed me, I didn't hide it and he didn't judge me (though he did boast A LOT). We encouraged each other and celebrated his success and supported my slower progress. When a few of the other kids saw this, they returned to try again, and soon I and a couple of the others were happily rolling wildly around on one wheel (though I never got as good as Robert). Kids of all ages have to know it's okay to be themselves, with all the ups and downs included, and that knowledge comes from YOU, which role you intend to play, and what impact you hope to have in the events that unfold.

So now you have a sense of who you are, who are the kids that are taking part?

WORKING *WITH* CHILDREN

To have any genuine impact, you will need to work *with* children and meet them at their level. The concept of agency is very important to understand when working with children: like anyone else, they should have the capacity to act independently and to make their own choices. This is key to the idea of "opt-in play", whereby children will willingly choose to take part in an activity. This doesn't mean that they won't sometimes hold back or that you won't occasionally need to encourage or gently push them toward taking on new challenges. But they will never offer you more than when you have earned their trust.

To do this, stay in the moment – and avoid making assumptions about anybody taking part. We sometimes create a narrative that this person is grumpy, or that person is shy. By reinforcing these traits, even if at one point they were evident, we actually make them in some way burdens that are very difficult for others to escape. Say, for example, your youngest once got upset at the age of six on a climbing wall, perhaps the family narrative has since become that the littlest doesn't like heights. While this might well come from a loving, protective and caring place, it could limit the child's opportunity for growth.

Courage is not the absence of fear; it is the will to go on despite it. Acknowledging the presence of personality traits without enforcing their continued impact is a tricky balance to achieve, but through play one that can be challenged. I cannot count how many times, through the delivery of the activities in this book, a parent has told me they are amazed "because little Jonathan is usually so shy", or "Amy never speaks up in school yet she told a joke on stage at a festival in front of everyone!" (See Kids' Comedy Corner, page 15.) The trick is to create as many possibilities and opportunities as we can through the non-judgemental playing of inclusive games.

Be open-minded; avoid generalizations or expectations about anybody's ability to take part based on their background. There's nearly always a way to overcome a challenge and every child, no matter who they are – rich, poor or any other sort of definition – will need the same level of attention and focus from you. At The Flying Seagull Project, part of the thrill of our work and the freedom of play is about breaking down obstacles. There have been numerous occasions when we've worked with children who have extreme mobility problems and, with a bit of imagination and determination, we have found a way to include them in the action so that, for instance, with support, a child who can barely walk has completed the high-wire challenge just like his classmates. And the same is true for all of us, whatever our age.

In 2008 I was working with a group of adults in Romania who had a wide range of disabilities. We were playing a musical game with clapping to create a rhythm, and everyone was asked to "offer" their name to the beat. The fourth person in the circle was a young man with speech difficulties, but with the help of the rhythm he was able to tell us his name was Stephen and then join in the rest of the session, calling out the audience responses that were part of the show. Afterwards, we sat down with the staff to discuss the session. They asked us in astonished voices how we'd managed to achieve what we had. It transpired that Stephen hadn't spoken for years when away from home. The answer was that we had simply played a game and he'd played too. We didn't assume he would; we didn't assume he wouldn't. We had offered an opportunity to him to take part – and he did.

It's amazing to see the look on the face of a child who now feels part of the community, having transcended any assumptions about them. This is one of the most important and powerful parts of our work. Your job as a parent or play-leader is to reveal that there are no limits, and to work together to find ways over apparent hurdles so that everyone can take part.

KIDS NEED RESPECT

Kids may be younger than adults and have seen less of the world; they may need our guidance and protection, but ... they also need respect!

Like many of us, when I was growing up I could not stand to be talked to like I was dumb by adults. Babyish voices, over-explanations – they drove me mad. Children are not lower status than adults and it's damaging to assume that they are. Meeting on a level of mutual respect can be incredibly beneficial for your relationship with your kids. This doesn't mean calling each other "mate", or that you are no longer in charge; what it means is that you honour them as having equal value to you. This is especially crucial in play, as this is their world!

In the world of play, assumed authority is illusory on the part of adults. That doesn't mean we're not in charge, and it doesn't even mean we can't demand that they take part in an activity in the way we want them to. The problem is that this sort of approach is not very much fun for anyone, and rather than empowering the children by helping them find their position within a societal group or community, it's more like disempowering them by making them comply to a subservient, dictatorial sort of approach.

That said, don't let them win every game or, if you do, at least make their victory believable! When you're sitting together don't do the adult thing of choosing a chair whilst they sit on the floor.

Keep To Your Word

Children deserve your full commitment. If a child asks you if you're going to play their favourite activity or game and you say "let's see" or "maybe", but you already know you won't, they will sense that gap. Then, you risk introducing an element of mistrust in your relationship. In the work of The Flying Seagull Project with communities of children in volatile situations, we learnt very quickly that even a throw-away promise can be remembered by them for years. Don't make a promise unless you know 100 per cent that you can and will deliver, and never underestimate the power of a promise kept – nor the damaging impact of one un-met.

Sit on the floor with them or give them all chairs. Ask them their opinions, and listen to them without criticism. If you disagree, have a discussion. Added together, these small things give a child a sense of importance and relevance, so they're not just passengers in an activity.

In the end this will lead to a self-confident, socially adjusted adult who is happy to discuss and who listens to others. Here lie the beginnings of a Real Play Revolution, in which the quality of play directly affects childhood and therefore transforms adulthood. With a world that's mostly out for itself, showing kids a bit of respect is not a bad way to start your own revolutionary action.

WHERE IT'S AT

Besides meeting the needs of participants, and accepting kids for who they are, when it comes to playing properly, there are logistical considerations to take into account, such as location.

Where is the game going to take place? There is a big difference, needless to say, between front-room Olympics and a game of Wink Murder in the school playing field. Whatever the space, be imaginative with it and use all its scope. For instance, if I was working with a group of kids in a large hall, I would set up different areas in the hall and take everyone on a journey between them. The opening circle would be located bang, smack in the middle of the space, with a short procession to a corner for music time, followed by a Mission Impossible wall sneak to the other side of the hall for a game of Grandmother's Footsteps, finishing with a sprint back again for a game of Bulldog. The entire session should be seamless play, not a series of games interspersed with pauses and logistical instructions.

If you're at home, how many rooms have you got to explore? Is there a garage, and drive, a loft or attic? Parents' rooms are traditionally a slightly more revered space, but could your room become part of your play tapestry?

Whatever space you use, keep it tidy. The minute you put something down, tidy it. The second somebody else goes off to another activity, tidy it. If there are toys all over the floor, you can't run around properly without the risk of breaking them. Also, if you've got a little one, it becomes even harder for them to join in if they are distracted by their surroundings. Tidy, tidy, tidy – and you will find the space you create rewards the effort.

When you are planning play, make sure you have all the resources that you need so that everyone has a chance of achieving the end goal that you have in mind. The end goal isn't about winning any prizes, but about the experience of participation itself. This does not mean reducing everything down to an activity that presents no challenges, or claiming "everyone's a winner"; rather, it's about redefining what participation means.

A COUPLE OF OTHER KEY COMPONENTS

To encourage everyone to take part, here are a couple of practical approaches to use, which play an important part in many of the games in this book:

- create a circle
- call and response.

CREATE A CIRCLE

A circle is by far the best shape to be working in, as everybody can see everyone else, no one is in the front or at the back, and it's easy to communicate with everybody simply by turning your head.

First of all, stand in the middle of the room where you wish to form the circle and call out, in a big, loud and tuneful voice, "Circle!" As people run over, hold out your hands to each side to encourage them to hold hands. Allow children to take your hands as the circle starts to form. Once it's nearly there, link the two hands on either side of you to each other and take your place in the middle of the circle. Move quickly into Call and Response (see below).

Then make sure the circle is equally spaced. If it's not, rather than ask individuals to move, use your eyes, expressions and gestures to encourage them to move around by following your example. Remember that this is already part of the game, so hide the technical and logistical elements with playful movements.

CALL AND RESPONSE

Call and Response is key to letting you know that children are engaged and willing to take part in an activity without being coerced. This ties in with the concept of "opt-in play" we touched on earlier, and it links into the idea of showing children respect. In order to teach our children that they have the right to stand at their full height, and to be deserving and demanding of respect from everybody in this world, both now and when they get older, it has to start here – with play. While we can order them to stand in a circle – or else! – it's far more appropriate if they stand in a circle because they were triggered by a vocal prompt that ignites a genuine desire to take part. Those children that we're working with should feel that they have a choice; that they have opted to take part in what we're doing and, as such, that they also have the right not to take part. Willing agreement is very important. When they have the choice – and particularly when that choice is presented as a game – it really changes the quality of what we're doing.

Call and Response is a vocally-led, physically-supported control technique. Now this might seem slightly sinister, but if you are working with a group of children or playing at home and there is no control, at some point this will result in the children being at risk or simply not having a fun experience. Call and Response invites them to give you their full attention so that you can lead any activities that follow. The idea is that they copy your words and gestures.

Here are two versions of Call and Response that I use when starting a games session.

1. *The Ballet Dancer*
    a. *Put both hands in the air and shout the word "HUP!"*
    b. *Make your fingertips touch each other, whilst slightly opening your arms at the elbows, and shout "HEY!"*
    c. *Lifting one leg off the ground, point the toe forward and shout "HO!"*
    d. *Bring the toe up to touch the side of the knee whilst shouting "HA!"*

    e. *Twirl around like a ballerina whilst singing in a silly voice the tune of the dance of the Sugar Plum Fairy.*

2. *The Teapot*
   a. *Put your hands straight up in the air, fast and energized, and shout the word "HUP!"*
   b. *Stick your hands out either side like a plane, and shout "HEY!"*
   c. *Leave your right arm sticking horizontally out, crook your left arm so that your fingertips touch your waist, making a handle shape, and shout "HO!"*
   d. *Raise your right hand slightly higher and draw the elbow in to resemble the spout of a teapot, whilst shouting "HA!"*
   e. *Slowly tilting your body in the direction of the spout, make the sound of a liquid pouring: "Blub, blub, blub, blub, blub!"*

Now, you can make your own Call and Response with any moves you like, but in order to make it serve the purpose of creating a framework where, when you say something, the children do as asked without it being a disciplinary exchange, keep it simple, energetic and easy to imitate.

As a version of Call and Response, I would suggest creating five or six mini chants that you can bust out whenever you feel like you want to pull the room back together, regain lost control, or simply pick the energy up.

THE END GOAL

What do the kids actually need from you? And what would you like them to achieve?

The end goal is one of the key elements in figuring out what you are offering them. The end goal in play can be as simple or complex as you wish, but it should be absolutely bespoke and custom-made for the children that you're working with.

If I'm working with a group of children who have come from a violent war-torn country and this is their first interaction with play since fleeing their homes, then my end goal will probably be something as absolutely simple as "I would like everybody to choose to join in the session." Now, whether the session is successful, and whether anybody even manages to play the game from start to finish, is not important. What is important is that I've set an end goal, an intention for the activity, and I will work toward it. Having thought about the background of the children and their specific needs, I tailor my end goal and my expectations realistically to match. It should be made up of three parts:

1. The practical aim: e.g. the kids physically take part.
2. The emotional aim: e.g. they feel confident enough to join in.
3. The lasting impact: e.g. they gain self-esteem and feel valued.

It is impossible to remain completely patient at all times, no matter how amazing you may be or how in love you are with the work you do or how passionate, encouraging and supportive you are. There will be times when the kids will push all your buttons and you will find it very difficult to keep a smile on your face. This is the moment when you reach inside and remember what your end goal is – and why you are working toward it.

If, for example, you're working with children who find it extremely difficult to remain in the circle or complete a challenge, one of the emotional offers you will have to make consists of patience, acceptance and forgiveness. In situations like this, it pays to celebrate small victories along the way. Imagine, for example, you have a couple of children in the group who, at first, are not able to join in the activities enjoyed by everyone else without arguing, fighting or becoming distracted. Perhaps even a month later they still won't play the whole game from beginning to end, but now when you ask everyone to form a circle, they join in straightaway and take part for five to ten minutes before losing their concentration. This progress represents a big success. (See also Keep Your Cool on page 139.)

ANONYMITY OF NONSENSE

The Anonymity of Nonsense is about creating an environment where everyone looks equally ridiculous. It's a great leveller if everybody looks totally silly: no matter how talented or good somebody is at mastering the rules, all the participants still look just as ludicrous as each other.

The purpose of this activity is to remove the pressure of having to achieve success or a certain standard, and instead replace these elements with a sense of irreverent fun and play.

You will need:
Face paints and weapons of decoration (e.g. sponges and small brushes)
Crazy hats, bow ties, wigs or other items of ridiculous clothing
Two chairs facing each other
A room full of willing players

Step 1. Ask everyone to sit in a circle: pretend to be outraged by their appearance. Say, for example, "How could you come here looking so sensible?" Then tell them you have a solution.

Step 2. Ask for a volunteer: gesture for him or her to take a seat in one of the chairs. With your face paints to hand, sit down facing them.

Step 3. Paint your volunteer's nose red: do this carefully, without saying a word. Next, purposefully place down the sponge and offer your nose to the volunteer for them to paint in return. Do all of this without speaking, as this makes the whole scenario far more enjoyable for all the participants. Once the volunteer has painted your nose, choose a different colour face paint and paint their cheeks; then allow them to do the same to you – and go back and forth until both your faces are painted. Finally, take a bow tie or other item and dress up the kid in it. Pop a hat or wig on their head. Then let them choose the same for you. By this point the group will be excited because they'll realize it's not gonna stop with one volunteer ...

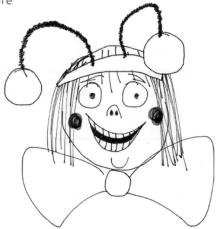

43

Step 4. Stand up: however, when the child tries to stand up too, beckon them to sit back down. Then take a place in the circle and, once again using gestures, encourage them to choose another volunteer from the group to take a seat and be painted. This process can be slow to begin with, but once everyone is used to what is happening, the sense of excitement starts to be replaced by impatience for their turn.

Step 5. Get everyone involved: it's crucial that everybody in the room receives the same red nose, bow tie and wig treatment – including all the adults present.

This is the Anonymity of Nonsense: even if you're good at the game, bad at it, usually confident or shy, once everyone has had their face painted and is wearing a ludicrous costume, you all become equally nonsensical and totally silly-looking.

Put the Focus on Taking Part

One of the most important roles that play has to offer us is the way it can establish a sense of equality. Whether we win or lose, the purpose of Real Play is participation, which allows us to feel part of something inclusive. It doesn't matter if we win or lose; what matters is that everybody has fun. All the same, while you can tell kids it's okay to lose and it's the taking part that counts, just saying those words alone will never convince a group of eight-year-olds that losing isn't a problem and winning doesn't matter. What you need to do, is to establish an environment in which the pressure is off and the game isn't all about gaining status over somebody else.

PLAY RULES AND THE GROWN-UP NAUGHTY STEP

If playing properly means accepting everyone as having an equal contribution to make to a game, then it only makes sense that children get to call the shots at times too.

Okay, I'm not suggesting that every household immediately installs a naughty step for grown-ups so that any time you do something your children don't like, they can punish you by making you sit on the step. Obviously on practical levels, such as when you quite reasonably refuse to feed them a chocolate-spread sandwich for dinner, this could turn into a disaster. However, there is something fun about changing the rules around in the time of play.

What I propose is that if you break a play rule, you consent to be sent to the naughty step. The play rules can be something that you agree together, and could include things like:

- agreeing to play properly by committing yourselves wholeheartedly to the game
- not looking at your mobile phone for the duration
- not chatting to the other grown-ups when you're meant to be playing
- a mandatory sub-clause that if you purposefully cheat in order to sit down for a few minutes, you have to stand on one leg instead.

Once you define a set of rules (see also page 152 for how to draw up Comedic Commitment Contracts), you then have to agree a process of discipline. For instance, two verbal warnings from the kids and the third time you're sent to the naughty step for a timeout. Not only does this create the sense that playtime is important, it also makes it clear that the usual hierarchy of the adults being in charge and kids having to follow their lead is

Any volunteers?

Choosing volunteers is very difficult to do well because if you pick someone who always gets chosen, you risk reaffirming for those who don't that the pattern will continue. However, if you start with a child who is slightly less forthcoming, you risk humiliating them or making them feel inhibited, so that they refuse to join in. Ideally, look for a confident member of the group, who is not the dominant leader or in any way claiming status over anybody else. It's okay to choose the class clown, as the clown within that child is not such a bad characteristic when engaged in positive activities.

removed during playtime. It invites us to play with the idea of authority by transferring the role of rule keeper and punishment distributor from the hands of the assumed leader, i.e. the adult, into the surprised hands of the newly empowered child. At the very least it's fun!

CALMING IT DOWN

One of the hardest things to get right is how to maintain discipline and keep games fun and flowing while at the same time acting like a responsible adult and making sure everything's fair. In many of the activities I talk about in this book, the focus is on increasing energy and volume while maintaining a high level of total chaos. When I use the word "chaos", however, I do not mean total disarray, which can lead to dominant kids taking over and less assertive kids being overlooked. What I do mean is the punk-like energy of being slightly WILD! As many of the games in this book encourage high energy, it's useful to have a fun way to pull a group back together in order to focus on the next activity.

UNITED WE CLAP!

This is a pretty good trick to pull everyone back to planet Earth and re-focus a group of kids. It's also a good way to end a play session.

Step 1. Make a circle: get everyone to stand shoulder to shoulder.

Step 2. Breathe: invite them to take a couple of deep, focusing breaths in and out.

Step 3. Explain the rules: using eye contact to hold their attention, explain that you are going to shout the word "hey" while clapping your hands and stamping. Their challenge is to clap, stamp and shout "hey" at exactly the same time you do. They will have to focus to try to sense exactly when you're about to make your move.

Step 4. Make your move: without any warning, shout "hey!" and clap and stamp just the once.

Step 5. Bring out their competitive streak: the first time you do this, there will be inevitably a gap between your movements and theirs. Feel free to tease them a little, telling them your granny moves faster! It might take a couple of rounds but I guarantee that pretty soon their competitive side will force them to scrutinize your every move, hoping to prove you wrong by clapping at the exact same time you do.

Step 6. Up the ante: if, after three or four rounds, your group is really focusing, give them some praise, as the challenge is about to get even harder. Tell them they have to close their eyes and close your own. Then repeat the exercise, squinting occasionally to make sure there are no cheaters. By this point, it should be almost silent in the room as everybody focuses intently on sensing the moment you clap.

Step 7. Wind it down: if the energy has refocused, end your session or move on to the next activity.

GAMES YOU GOTTA PLAY PROPERLY

Here is a handy kitbag of games to invite commitment and focus from all the players.

GAME 1: WINK MURDER

This is a game that requires concentration and conspiracy – and good old-fashioned humour.

You will need:
Seven or more participants
Enough space to form a tight circle
Cunning

Step 1. Make a circle: ask everyone to choose one of the players in the circle to be a police detective. The police detective then leaves the room. (If that's not an option, distract the detective by making lots of noise or spinning them round with their eyes closed.)

Step 2. Choose the wink murderer: while the detective is out of the room (or otherwise engaged), the circle chooses another person to play the murderer. When the police detective returns to the circle, the wink murderer is going to wink at people to "murder" them while avoiding detection. To add to the theatricals, offer a prize to the most elaborate and over-the-top death! Your group must also try to be subtle and not stare openly at the killer.

Step 3. Let the investigation begin: the police detective comes back into the room... Terrible news! A killer is on the loose and the detective only has three tries to guess who it is. To guess, they have to name the killer, but if they are wrong they lose a try.

Step 4. Solve the murder: When the detective names the wink murderer or runs out of tries, play another round until more of you have had a go at being either the detective or the murderer.

You can play a variation of Wink Murder called Murder on the Dance Floor. Played to music, everybody mimics the crazy dance moves of the murderer, while the dance detective has to guess who he or she is. If you have players with limited mobility, they can use clapping and slapping knees etc. The actual movement is not the important bit; rather, it's about focus.

GAME 2: JACOB'S LADDER

This game is the human equivalent of the wooden children's toy, and involves a lot of running about and high energy, as well as complete concentration to avoid accidents and penalty points.

You will need:
Eight or more players (in pairs)
Someone to call out the numbers
Space to sit in a long line and run beside it
Precision and speed

Step 1. Create the ladder: each pair sits facing each other, with the soles of their feet flat against each other to form the rungs of Jacob's ladder. Between each pairing, there should be around a metre of space. Starting at the top pair, number each partnership; then make sure they know their numbers by asking them to shout it out.

Step 2. Call out the pairs by number: when you call out a number, the corresponding partnership leaps up and runs as fast as they can, jumping over the rungs of the ladder to reach the top. Then they run all the way back down the outside, before leaping over the bottom rungs of the ladder (if necessary) to make their way back to their original space. The person who sits down first wins three points for their team. The two teams are formed by the left side of the ladder versus the right side of the ladder.

Step 3. Avoid accidents through penalties: there is a catch – there are five penalty points, or minus points, for accidentally kicking or landing on one of the rungs. So your team could be worse off if you go too fast and accidentally tread on someone. It is worth explaining this, as the result will be that though they compete and go as fast as they can, they will also be super focused on not connecting with anybody else or accidentally hurting them.

Step 4. Play the game in four rounds: at the start of each fresh round, remind each team that accidentally stepping on or kicking anyone else leads to five penalty points. In the first round, call out each number slowly and wait until each partnership has made it back to their original place. In the second round, call out each number slightly more quickly and start the next couple off before the earlier team have made it back to their place. In the third round, explain that the first two rounds have only been practice runs – and now we're really going to play! The third round is fast. Call out the numbers so that they are jumbled up. The result will be mild chaos and lots of laughter.

Step 5. Create total carnage: In the fourth round, explain that now you really mean it, and there are no more practice rounds. Call out the numbers as fast as you can, starting with the highest number and ending with the lowest. There will be total chaos, which will eventually organize itself back into a very wonky ladder. At this point, start again, only calling out the lowest numbers first as fast as you can, which will result in even more chaos – and a very happy, very silly way to end the game.

GAME 3: GRANDMOTHER'S FOOTSTEPS

This is a really good game to help regain focus in a group. Introduce this game in the hushed, exciting and sneaky voice that befits the challenge to follow. The volume should go right down to a whisper. There may be some giggles; however the noise and energy should be intensely focused.

You will need:
Eight or more players
Enough space to sneak at least 12 uninterrupted paces
Spy-like sneakiness

Step 1. Explain the rules: one person (you the first time round) is going to be Grandmother while the children line up by the far wall or a short distance away. (You can change the name of the game to suit the circumstances; at Halloween, for instance, I would call it Dracula's Footsteps.) Explain in simple terms: "When I face the opposite direction, you have to try to sneak up and tap me on the back. However, when I look round, you must freeze on the spot like a piece of stone. If I look and you move or make a noise, you have to go all the way back to the beginning and try again. The only rule is no running! That's because it's too easy for me when you run as you can't stop in time and it's easy to see you move."

Step 2. Start the game: when a child reaches you and taps you successfully on the back, they are to shout out their name. At this point they become the grandmother/Dracula/bank manager, while you join the rest of the group for round two.

Step 3. Create mischief: when I play the grandmother, I like to try to trick the children into moving. I've warned them beforehand that whatever I say, whatever I do, they mustn't move a muscle. Then I yell things like "watch out, there's a snake!" or "hands up if you didn't move" – whatever it takes to get them to move. If you want, you can even use props like a feather duster to tickle their noses to make them move or giggle.

You probably only want to play this game three or four times, but it's a great way to change the atmosphere and dynamic of a group, especially if it's the end of playtime and you're going to go in the house, get your pyjamas and go to bed!

THE IMPACT OF PLAYING PROPERLY

My work with The Flying Seagull Project has brought home to me how important it is to be completely present in every single second, with every individual child, in everything I do – from the smallest gesture to the loudest noise I make. Being 100 per cent genuine is the only truly successful method. I call it the spinning-plate technique. Every player or participant is like a spinning plate and will need your energy to start spinning, and for you to look after them individually so they don't fall.

I set myself a challenge that each and every child leaves the activity believing they are special. This only needs some really genuine eye contact and a moment where you "see" them fully. It can be a tiring and sometimes intensely demanding way to work, but when you are dealing with the souls of young people, and offering stimulus that may weave itself into their hopes and dreams for the future, I believe that anything short of everything doesn't cut it!

Whoever you are and whatever the location, if you are engaging with kids, you need to know what it is that you're taking with you and to be able to adapt your expectations to their reality, which means your plans should include a degree of flexibility. Whether you're playing a game of rounders or baseball, or running around in the woods, or simply doing a dressing-up game, everything needs to have been thought through first; so that, for example, you have a fast version, a slow version, and a total abandon-the-game-for-Plan-B option.

That said, as we've seen, practicalities are only one part of it: the spine-tingling, sense-shaking, dream-building experience of Real Play is not achieved by adults being clever and controlling details. For Real Play, we have to commit ourselves to it wholeheartedly.

CHAPTER 3

LET GO

"If in doubt, smile and shout - fun is what it's all about!"

Sometimes it's fun to choose to lose and let go ... By this, I don't mean refusing to play properly by holding back. I mean lose your ego, lose your inhibitions, lose your embarrassment – lose the plot! Make the experience the important bit, rather than getting hung up on the outcome. As mentioned, non-competitiveness is an essential quality of Real Play. This doesn't mean you can't have fun playing tennis with your kids, but if you are striving to achieve something particular within that experience, it stops being play and becomes sport instead. As we've seen, the fantastic thing is that when we play properly, it's inclusive of all abilities and interests. This is why we need to reframe the idea of winning and losing. Too often we attach adult values to play, linking it to a sense of achievement or a gauge of worth. This is something I am inherently against, as I think play should literally be for its own sake.

It's been said that play is the highest form of research, and this is especially the case in childhood. Yet, while we know that play is to do with developing social bonds and learning about our strengths and risks, there should be no need for us to focus deliberately on these aspects, as they will occur naturally when we play properly. For play to be a genuine experience, we must make sure that any agenda or desirable outcome happens as the by-product rather than as a focus of what we plan to do. This is partly what I mean when I say "let go": let go of everything you know, everything you think about yourself, all your inhibitions, and everything you think a game should include.

In this chapter, I have some pretty radical and slightly wild ideas for you. These will take you to the edge where you can test out boundaries and broaden horizons. It's time to set yourself free and become the spark that sets them on fire ...

UNLEASH THE BEAST ART ATTACK

This game is a great way to put inhibitions to one side and to overcome shyness and embarrassment. It's all about giving ourselves permission to express ourselves in any way we choose, without worrying about being judged or being "good enough". It works for adults and children, whether in groups or by themselves.

You will need:
Overalls or old clothing to wear
Very old footwear that you can splash paint on (or shoes covered in taped-up plastic bags)
A plastic shower cap
Eye protection (swimming goggles will do)
Water-soluble paints in different colours and various pots to decant them into
Paper to paint on (the reverse of old wallpaper will do)
Masking tape (optional)
Anything you can mobilize paint with: from a traditional paintbrush to a tennis ball tied to a rope, a piece of sponge stuck on a stick to a mop – the more elaborate and unusual the better

Space where you can make mess, such as part of the garden or the garage
Loud music to paint to (protect the music system in plastic so it won't get damaged)

Step 1. Prepare your weapons of mass disruption: pour the paints into trays and pots along one side of the space where you'll be working. On the other side, lay out your "brushes": basically anything that it might be fun to paint with. Set out your paper. If you have easels, great; if not, a table covered in paper would be perfect. Or lay it on the ground. Use the masking tape to stick the paper in place if necessary, and have more paper readily to hand.

Step 2. Get the music ready: now the focus is not on what you paint, but on how it feels to paint. This activity is going to be somewhere between a dance, an explosion and an outpouring, using a fresh sheet of paper for each of the three stages. The first track of music should be quite fast; the second track should be something a little slower; and the third absolutely manic.

Step 3. Unleash the beast and get painting: turn on the first track of music and, using your "brushes" or even your hands, begin to fling paint around – at the paper, not at each other! The only rule is that nobody is allowed to attack anyone else with paint, because even if in jest, the result will be a paint fight, which is not what this is about.

Step 4. Admire your handiwork: to sustain the energy and to stop everyone from getting fussy and critical over their creations, the entire process shouldn't last more than 20 minutes. At the end, you may have some artwork that you would like to keep, but it doesn't matter if you end up throwing the whole lot in the bin. Or you could use them to make a "zine" (see page 60).

Sometimes, getting out there, getting messy, getting noisy, getting in the rioters, and unleashing some of the inner turmoil and the inner crazy that we've learned from a very young age to

keep square, is an extremely healthy release and a way to get rid of some of those inner tensions.

UNLEARNING WHAT WE'VE BEEN TOLD IS TRUE

At some point between childhood and adulthood, we begin to believe that if we're not very good at something, we shouldn't really be doing it – even if that activity was initially just for fun, even if we never intended to make it our profession, or we just enjoyed doing it occasionally with a couple of mates in the garden and it made us laugh. Whether the pressure comes from society or our friends, it still feels very real. Yet it truly doesn't matter if we're good at something or not: if we enjoy doing it, that is the only reason we need.

There are those of us who are lucky enough to follow the career path that also represents our hearts' desires. (I know I'm lucky that there isn't a job I can think of that I'd rather be doing than the one I have.) However, too many of us end up following a career path that, over the years, takes up an ever-increasing amount of our time, while also demanding more and more of our energy. This, coupled with only focusing on those pursuits that we are naturally good at, means we often only take part in activities that are either professionally necessary for us or because we want to become even better at them. We miss out on the relaxation of Real Play.

When a child of five, say, makes a squawk on a trumpet, that noise already represents a huge achievement. But as adults, it's not quite so easy for us to take up something new: we can be overcome with embarrassment when we realize we're awful at it, at least to start with. As adults, we're not used to doing things that we're bad at, especially in public. However, if we're working with children, it's essential for us to let go of the notion of perfection and to dig deep and find that inner chaos.

Most of the time, a child is always on the verge of running, jumping, hollering or yelling. At least if that child is lucky enough to grow up in an environment that allows her to express herself freely. The uninhibited nature of children is their default position until society comes crashing down on them. However, as adults, only occasionally do we let those walls down; and only then do we find that we can act as crazy or as loud or uninhibited as we once were when we too were little.

While our role as responsible adults means we can't always hare around like space cowboys in the garden, there is still a necessity to "unleash the beast" at times and to overcome our inner inhibitions – especially if we wish to connect with kids and enjoy healthy interactions with them. And who knows what exciting new qualities we might discover in ourselves if we let go of our old ways of thinking about who we are and how we ought to behave?

SCRIBBLE-SESSION LIGHTNING ZINE

I love art, and I love drawing. Yet, in traditional terms, you could say I'm absolutely terrible at it. Like me, many of the kids that I work with find it difficult to draw a picture. And if I were to give them a piece of paper and tell them to draw anything they want, they would still ask me, "What?"

This is where scribble art comes in: it's another great activity that focuses on the importance of the process rather than on perfecting a skill. It was taught to me by Harriet, a tattooed skateboarder, who shares her passion for art in her work with children. With scribble art, there is no "what"; there is simply "how". In this particular activity, it creates the materials for making a zine or miniature magazine. (As you will need to use a craft knife to make the zine, this activity is best suited to older kids.)

You will need:
A rectangular sheet of paper
Hand-held weapons of scribble, i.e. felt-tip pens, pencils and crayons
A pen, pencil or fine-tipped permanent marker (a Sharpie is ideal) for writing down words or thoughts
A surface to work on
Music
A ruler, cutting mat and a craft knife (to be used under supervision as necessary)

Step 1. Get moving: first, you want to wake up everyone's body, and get that sense of liberation and playful silliness into the room. I recommend One Minute Madness (see page 81) for this.

Step 2. Get ready: ask everybody to pick a handful of pens and crayons, take a sheet of paper and find a place to work. Where possible, it's best if participants can stand while they scribble, but if that's not possible for any reason, then it's perfectly fine to be seated.

Step 3. Liberate the scribble: make an impassioned and slightly comedic speech to explain that everyone is going to cover their piece of paper with the coloured pens and pencils. Tell them that pictures aren't important, style is not important, colours are not important – they are the only thing that matters! Play music to raise the energy (see Unleash the Beast Art Attack on page 56, and try using three different short tracks to vary the tempo).

Step 4. Keep the scribbling short and sweet: this is not meant to be a long exercise. After a minute or two, invite them to place their sheet of scribble onto the floor and start a new one, till they have about three sheets. Keep encouraging them to express themselves in any way they choose, using any number of pens and any style of drawing, mark-making or scribbling.

Step 5. Time to zine: a zine is a miniature magazine in which you can write whatever you like. To make the zine, take one of the scribbled sheets of paper and, following the steps below and the diagram overleaf, fold it up:

a. *Position the paper so it's horizontal and fold it in half, lining up the two long edges.*
b. *Now, fold it in half vertically so that the two short edges meet up.*
c. *Fold it in half again vertically, making the two short edges meet up.*
d. *Unfold the paper, which is now divided into eight sections.*
e. *Using the craft knife and ruler, cut a horizontal slit where the two vertical middle sections meet, so you have a sort of letterbox opening.*

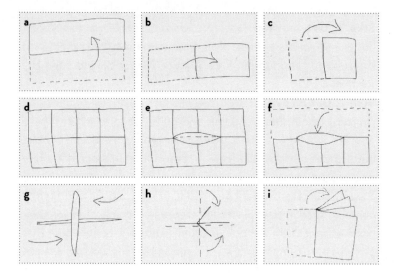

f. Fold the paper along the same horizontal line again, so that the two long edges of the sheet meet up.

g. Push the two side panels toward each other as if you were playing the accordion, so that the slit opens in a sort of square beak.

h. Then close the beak so that the paper now looks like a cross from above.

i. Take the top and left-hand arm of the cross and fold them over to the right, so they sandwich the two other arms. Press down on the spine of your booklet.

You now have a zine with eight blank sides on which to make your mark!

If it doesn't work the first time, just take another sheet of scribble and try again!

Step 6. Say what you wanna say: encourage everyone to think about what they want to put in their zine. It could be a story, a poem, a list of their favourite words, a recipe, a description of their favourite book or holiday, pictures on top of pictures, a sketch of an amazing new invention, a design for a perfect robot, a map from their house into space – you get the idea! Offer as many different suggestions as you can. Then ask them to write or draw it, using the pens.

Step 7. Get your zine into circulation: the final step is to give the zine to somebody else as a gift. A bit like a magazine has readers, choose somebody who you feel would like to read or receive your zine. (And because it's only scribbles and folded into a form of booklet, nobody will feel sad if it doesn't get put on the wall.)

Zines can be themed very easily and make great personalized alternatives to greetings cards. Can you imagine anything more touching than receiving a homemade zine on Mother's Day?

OLD CLOTHES, NEW CLOTHES

Defeating the ego is a challenge for all of us. When I say "ego", I'm not just talking about the part of us that wants to show off, but which also acts as a self-defence: the ego is linked to shyness just as much as it is to being overbearing.

Knowing that we are good enough as we are is part of letting go and overcoming the ego. And I believe that letting go of the need to look good, or to have the right things, is an important part of childhood. It is our job as parents and play leaders to go one step further than simply telling children, "Of course you're good enough, it doesn't matter what you look like, it doesn't matter what anybody else thinks of you." We have to find easy and trustworthy ways to show that this truly is the case.

Nothing highlights this better than when we see somebody who is acting completely out of the norm and having a fantastic time doing so: humour and comedy are essential in the art of self-effacement. So this quick tip is about mixing up what we wear.

Have you noticed how when kids do stuff like climb trees, they are nearly always dressed in old clothes such as blue jeans, trainers and some sort of old T-shirt or plaid shirt? Obviously this makes sense, but what if we were to reverse some of the norms and do something a bit different? Charity and thrift shops sell formal clothes at very low prices. What if when we went to climb trees, rather than wearing a pair of denim jeans and a shirt, we wore a three-piece suit? Now, I hear the answer is that it wouldn't be very easy to climb in clothes like that – but nor would it be in tight jeans if you think about it. What if you said, "Okay kids,

get your rough clothes on", and as a family of four you went out wearing three-piece suits? Yes, it's total nonsense, and I'm not suggesting you do it every day, but sometimes the act of making complete fools of ourselves in a way that is undeniably funny and exciting can be a fantastic tool for undoing some of the pressures of perfection. Instead, if we challenge the norms occasionally, we teach our children to question some of the expectations that society has of us, and to choose their own way through life.

GOOD GAMES TO LET GO!

Here is a selection of games that will help everyone to lose their inhibitions and join in the fun.

GAME 1: TUNNELS

Tunnels is simple but one of the craziest and funniest games you play, especially if the participants are all different sizes. But do advise them to take care so that nobody is accidentally bumped into and hurt when they are crawling through each other's legs.

You will need:
12 or more players, split into two teams
Enough space for the teams to line up
Meerkat-like burrowing talent

Step 1: Get in position: the two teams each form a line, standing close enough so that they can place their hands on the shoulders of the person in front of them. Legs are apart to form the tunnel.
Step 2: Choose the team's arrival call: every time a competitor completes the challenge, they have to make a sound. This can be a roaring cow's moo, a squawking peacock call or whatever takes your fancy.
Step 3: On your marks, get ready ...: starting with the person at the back, each competitor has to crawl through the opened legs of their team-mates. When they reach the end of the tunnel, they

stand up straight and become the front of the line. The person at the back then begins the same process.

Step 4: Shout out for the champions: once the entire team has made it from back to front, to claim their place as the champions they simply have to sit down, cross their arms and legs and make the team noise together.

GAME 2: AMOEBA TAG

For many years now I have led a passionate campaign against the game of Tag, also known as It. This, in my opinion, is not a game; it's something kids do until they can come up with a better game to play. Also, there's nearly always one kid who has a special technique, such as holding their arms out wide so that every time you get them, they merely tag you straight back – and this sort of smug, under-engaged style of playing really bugs me! So the Flying Seagull Project has adopted an advanced version called Amoeba Tag.

You will need:
Eight or more participants
Enough space to run around without bumping into each other
Quick moves and fast hands

Step 1: Choose two amoeba: the game begins with two separate amoeba, whose job is to grab or touch the other participants and add them to their creation by shouting, "Consumed!" The two amoeba run around while everyone else tries to avoid capture.

Step 2: Growing the amoeba: once an amoeba has tagged another person, they then hold hands and become part of the amoebae. The amoebas keep going until everybody has been caught or time is up.

Step 3: The biggest amoeba wins: the winning team has the most people in their creature. The punishment of the team that loses, is to be encircled and eaten by the other team. They can do this through something silly like tickling them, giving them a high five or a squeeze. (If you're playing with a particularly energetic group, it's worth making it clear what "eating" means in this instance!)

GAME 3: STUCK IN THE MUD

An oldie but a goldie, Stuck in the Mud is always lots of fun and a game that we must never let disappear. I read somewhere that children are no longer allowed to crawl underneath each other's legs and instead are supposed to play this game by running under raised arms. Let me be perfectly clear: that is complete rubbish, and something to be healthily ignored. What I would say is to encourage your teams to aim low when crawling to avoid any sort of injury.

You will need:
Five or more players
Enough space to run around without crashing into each other
High speed – and a wide stance!

Step 1. Choose your mud monster: depending on the size of the group, I would recommend having one mud monster to every ten players. The mud monster's goal is to tag and thereby en-mud or "stick" each and every member of the group.

Step 2. Everyone else flees from the mud monster: as soon as a runner is touched by the mud monster, that runner is immediately stuck in the mud. To be stuck in the mud means you stand with your arms and legs open wide and you are no longer able to move until somebody de-freezes you.

Step 3. Free people who are stuck: to be freed, one of your team-mates simply has to crawl or wriggle as low as possible between your legs. Once free you can then run on and of course help your other team-mates in the same way by going through their legs.

Step 4. Create more monsters: after the first few rounds it can be quite fun to "silly-up" the challenge by saying, for example, that everybody wearing red is now a mud monster, or all the girls or all the boys, or everyone who likes marmite. It becomes really fun when huge numbers have to chase huge numbers. This means the game is over quickly but ends in lots of giggles.

LETTING IN THE ENERGY

Play is not about the creative management of a child's time; Real Play is the total engagement of a child's imagination. Play is where children weave the tapestry of their dreams, and get to be anything and everything they want. Play is where there is no too tall, too small, too slow, too fast, not clever enough, not dressed right or not confident enough! Play includes none of this, as it is a universal feeling of liberation, creativity and expression.

In this way, play supersedes the ego. As we have seen, for a parent or anybody else engaging with children in a playful way, it is vital to put aside the agenda of your own ego and ideas. It is essential to get down on the lawn and muddy your knees; to put yourself on the line and make a fool of yourself, and actively play with children rather than attempt to guide or manage their activities from the sidelines.

There is, moreover, something extremely revealing about playing in this way: it is the ultimate act of improvisation and test of self-esteem (for an adult at least). But the fantastic thing about playing like this, is that it also allows us to break free of the definitions of who and what we are. This experience can offer a deep sensory freedom which can undo and heal many of the tensions we might be carrying around with us as adults.

When we put aside our ego and inhibitions, Real Play frees us up and allows us to step into the energy of the moment – something that we're going to be looking at more closely next.

CHAPTER 4

GET ENERGIZED

"Energy is contagious..."

It doesn't matter how many times I say it, it's always worth repeating: it's not what you do that is important, but the energy with which you do it. Whether you're working in a professional capacity with kids or simply trying to be a good parent, energy is probably the most important resource you have – and ironically the one that's hardest to maintain 24/7. Communication with children is more than 80 per cent non-verbal and, unlike adults who learn to take words at face value, or at least to ignore that feeling of discomfort when words and feelings are out of sync, kids can't or won't accept this. This also means that, unlike adults, they are by virtue of their very nature less inclined to accept untruths and misleading authority figures – which is important to bear in mind when it comes to the example that we set for them as they grow up. For kids, the energy in any given activity has to resonate authentically on all levels for the duration.

I believe in making most games turbocharged so that whatever difficulties, insecurities, or troubles our children may be experiencing, they are liberated from its heaviness through play –

and by the transformative energy that play creates when done properly. As everyone knows, growing up isn't easy, even when we seem to have all the creature comforts and family support that we could ask for. There will still be discomfort simply because whenever we experience the world anew – which we do almost every day as a child – this entails a degree of fear, confusion and, at times, bewilderment. Play is the safe haven where we can entirely immerse ourselves in the secure world of make-believe. This is why it's so important to use your energy to enwrap the participants in your games in such a strong, warm and loving energy that everything else vanishes.

Over the past decade or so, The Flying Seagull Project has taken this to the next level by working with children living in dangerous environments. We have worked on the borders of Greece and Macedonia, for example, when the European Union shut the door to refugees and almost 20,000 people were forced to live in a field on the border. This place was toxic! There were police, the army, mafia, traffickers, fascists and every different type of desperate person you can imagine. Most days, fights and violence were not just possible, they were expected. The air was rarely free from the smell of tear gas, and mixed with the ever-increasing desperation to cross the border, the energy of this camp became stifling enough to make even the most confident of people feel claustrophobic and trapped.

In the middle of all of this were 3,000 children, who needed a different energy to survive. Never before, or arguably since, have I been so utterly convinced that positive energy can change the world, having seen with my own eyes how the atmosphere of an entire camp became transformed. When we entered the camp in the mornings, the oppression and fear that followed another night of violence hung thick in the air, and worry was visible on the stressed faces of the people. Even the children looked like worn-out old folk. However with some big, loud, loving energy, we were able to transform the atmosphere into one that felt like playtime within just a few minutes. We'd call for a circle, and the children would come running from their makeshift tents. When they held hands and looked up to see our energized faces, they visibly returned to childhood. Colour would literally flush back into their faces, and the sparkle of play would glint from their eyes. Even if it was only for that half an hour, the world became wonderful, safe, playful and loving – and most importantly it became inclusive of them!

Part of our job was to raise the volume both vocally and physically to such an exaggerated extent that we could drown out the din and racket of the rest of the camp. We'd push the noises of the police, helicopters and continued shouting to the edges of the field, and within our circle together we'd create the sound of singing, applause and laughter. Energy, when rightly delivered, can transform the way a person feels – from the top of their head to the tips of their toes.

Obviously the situation I've described is extreme; however, I would argue that there is never a day when being surrounded by really robust and positive energy doesn't feel good, and isn't needed. If you wake up in the morning, come downstairs and see the person with whom you share your home smiling from ear to ear and they wrap you in a positive and loving energy with a huge good morning, how could that ever be bad? There's no such thing as too much happiness, or feeling too safe.

We all know that unavoidable dangers, unavoidable losses and unavoidable suffering are simply a part of life. While there is little we can do about this, we can change the way each day feels by pumping positive energy into every single moment. In this chapter, I'm going to share a few exercises and games that never fail to raise the heartbeat and lift the vibe until it can feel like it's carnival day every day of the week.

> # Shout It Out!
>
> One thing to try when playing with children is simply to yell the word "ENERGY!" and see how dynamically they reply. The chances are they will shout the word right back at you – and everyone will feel it.

ROCK YOUR SOCKS OFF DRUM COMPETITION

This can be a simple, spontaneous half-hour game, or as involved as you like, with a few weeks of preparation and invites to other families and groups to get them to join in too. You could spice up a summer barbecue by adding this as a theme: it would give the kids something to do and will definitely open communication with your neighbours!

Most importantly the Rock Your Socks Off Drum Competition will generate a unique and eccentric energy that the kids will remember for a long time afterwards with a smile. In the end, isn't that what it's all about?

You will need:

A few daft dressing-up props, such as giant sunglasses, headbands, torn denim etc. (optional)
Drum kit made out of any items that can be whacked, such as old pots, pans or whatever else you have to hand
A music system and a collection of at least ten classic 80s' and 90s' rock tracks (think Motorhead, Van Halen, AC/DC)
Cucumbers to present to the semi-finalists
Earplugs!

Step 1. Make a drum kit: before the game, you can ask the players to help you make a homemade drum kit out of pots and pans, etc. Place it where it will be stable so that it can be thwacked without limits. It's the going-wild element of this game that makes it work.

Step 2. Dress the part: get the competitors to dress up in bits of rocker's attire, such as sunglasses and bandanas, etc.

Step 3. Share some catchphrases: teach everyone catchphrases to yell during each round. Give these a try (borrowed from Seagulls' member "Rock Star Andy"):

You: To those of you about to rock... *Kids:* We salute you!

You: Who we gonna stick it to...? *Kids:* The man!

You: What are you gonna do...? *Kids:* Rock our socks off!

You: That solo was so hot... *Kids:* It melted our faces!

Step 4. Master the moves: you ain't a rock star until you master the classic moves of rock. Looking like a rock star is half the battle. Gather your rockers in the "Circle of Rock" and teach them the basics in the style of a martial arts class. Once you've shown them each move, call out the moves for them to perform as if testing a series of karate kicks and throws.

- *Power slide on two knees*: taking care of the knees, run and slide on two bended knees, hands flung skyward and head back.
- *Bull horns*: this is a hand gesture more than a move – using your thumb to hold down your middle two fingers, point your index and little finger to the sky on both hands.
- *Classic headbang*: a classic bit of front to back power nodding, aka headbanging.
- *Head down stadium point*: stand with both legs wide, one hand down with splayed fingers, the other arm straight up with one finger pointing to the sky. The head should be down as if humbly accepting the total worship of your adoring fans.

Step 5. Get the show on the road with a spot of air guitar: find out who will be crowned the "Ruler of Rock" and who the "coolest cucumbers" are (the runners-up). To decide the order, have a an "air-guitar off" to a couple of tracks, picking the wildest contender to kick off proceedings. (This is also a good way to ensure you don't pick someone who isn't confident enough to go first.)

Step 6. Start the drum competition: invite the first contender up and tell them they have 15 seconds to show the drum kit who's boss. Introduce the first catchphrases here: e.g. ask the contender, "Who are you gonna stick it to...?" Then turn to the audience and chant, "For those of you about to rock..." Lower the music volume, hand them the sticks and step back. If they need encouragement to get going, give it to them to encourage an outburst of madness on the drums! Once they finish, go wild with praise. Then it's time for the next contender, until everyone has had a go. (If there are other grown-ups present, make sure at least a couple of them take part too.)

Step 7. Choose the semi-finalists: pick at least three of the maddest drummers to take part in the semi-finals. Keep on using the catchphrases, asking for the rocker's moves, calling at the audience to do bull horns (see page 75) and generally allowing everyone to get carried away with the fun.

Step 8. Choose the finalists: once the semi-finalists have had another short go, ask the audience to decide the two finalists using a "clapometer", screaming and shouting when you lift the hopefuls' arms up. Award a "cucumber of cool" to those semi-finalists who don't make it through to the finals. (I know the cucumber-trophy thing sounds weird, but there's something so utterly silly about

an actual cucumber that it works!)

Step 9. Choose the champion: the final two contenders will have only ten seconds to perform and once again will be voted on by the crowd. The ultimate winner gets to do a musical victory lap, playing along to their favourite classic rock track. Turn up the volume and encourage the crowd to leap up and rock out, using their rocker's moves and promising to award more cucumbers for the crazy cats!

Hype the Hyperbole!

There's nothing wrong with a little bit of hyperbole, or even wild exaggeration, for the purposes of comedy. Let rip: "That's the world's most perfect circle!" "That's the slowest I've ever seen anyone move in the history of all things!" "This is the greatest moment of the entire millennia!" It adds dynamic energy to exaggerate everything. Which is why I would encourage you to try for every single second of every single day for the rest of your lives to include a little bit of casual wild exaggeration...Trust me, it will get them giggling.

COUNTDOWN TO BLAST OFF!

Five, four, three, two, one! This is a countdown. Yes, I know you knew that – but did you know that a countdown is one of the most effective ways to get a group of children to listen and follow your lead?

An energetic countdown can be a fun and useful tool to move everyone swiftly from one activity to another. For example, if you've been playing a game of Stuck in the Mud (see page 67), but now you want everyone to return to the circle, all you need to do is to run to the centre of where the circle will be, shout, "Okay, you have just ten seconds to make the world's most perfect circle – ten, nine, eight, seven..." by which point the children will be racing to make that circle. They are doing exactly what you have requested them to do, but with the energy and intention of a game or challenge. This is another good example of the "opt-in" philosophy: they're choosing to make the circle, and choosing to do it quickly, without you having to say anything as boring as "hurry up or else". You simply do a countdown.

I recommend always counting down fewer numbers than there is actually time to do something; for example, give them ten seconds to do something that you know will take 30. This means they have to be fast. However, it also means you have to be inventive when you get down to number one (I often end up saying "one" 20 or 30 times). Another option is to count down from one to a half, to a quarter to an eighth, to 16th to a smidgen to a tiny bit, to an infinitesimal fraction to a microscopic dot to a semi-atomic nothingness ... All of this whilst increasing the intensity, energy and urgency of your voice.

QUICK 'N' QUIRKY QUIZ

Ignore the word "quiz" and all the notions of mundanity and passivity that it usually evokes. I'm obviously not talking about that kind of game here. This high-energy version is played on your feet, and involves fun facts that'll frazzle your brain!

You will need:

Space to run from one side of the area, which represents "true", to the other, which is "false"

Something with which to make a countdown sound, such as a drum roll or fast music or just your voice

Something to make a crash noise with: ideally a cymbal, but a frying pan hit with a spoon will do

At least 20 quirky "facts", of which ten should be real and ten made up

Step 1. The quiz master explains the rules: one side of the room or area represents "false", while the other is "true". If contenders think a statement is true, they should run to the "true" side, and if they think it's false, they should go to the "false" side. They will have only ten seconds to make up their minds and after that they can't change their answer. The statements have got to be quirky enough to hold their attention and a mix of easy and hard.

Step 2. Get the game started: ask your first question and ask the players to decide their answer by running to either the "true" or "false" area. During the ten seconds they have to decide, play the drum roll or fast music.

Step 3. Complete the round: once the time is up, crash the cymbal, then repeat the initial question and reveal the answer.

Step 4. Start the next round: if playing to pick a winner, the kids who choose the right answer get to stay on for the next round. Yell, "Back in the middle for another riddle!" Once the kids with the wrong answers are out, they can act as a highly vocal advice board, yelling suggestions to those still playing. Carry on until you have a clear winner or you run out of questions. Simply playing for the fun of it is perfectly fine, without aiming for a champion.

Here are some example questions from my quiz:
True or false: a polar bear has white fur.
Answer: False, their fur is transparent, like fiber optic tubes that take on the colour of their surroundings.
True or false: a circus ringmaster wears a shiny baseball cap.
Answer: false, ringmasters wear top hats!
True or false: elephants can't jump.
Answer: true!
True or false: The American government, in partnership with NASA, spliced the DNA of a spider and a goat to create a spider goat, whose milk came out like a web and was used to make space rockets and bullet-proof vests?
Answer: true!

Run the first couple of rounds yourself and then appoint another quiz master to take over. Everyone will enjoy the freaky facts!

RUBBER CHICKEN

A high-speed way to go from 0 to 60 in energy is to play the game Rubber Chicken. It is essentially a movement exercise but encourages outrageous amounts of noise and short bursts of chaos. If you are gathered in a circle in a cold room, are playing late in the day, are about to start or finish a long journey or if there is any other reason why the energy is flat, Rubber Chicken is the perfect way to wake everybody up. I would recommend doing this activity at the beginning of a play session, and to offer a small, fun reward for the rubberiest chicken. Something like the first biscuit in the break, the comfiest seat on the couch or the window seat on a long journey.

It works like this: everyone counts loudly from one to eight while shaking an arm as if trying to flick water off their fingers. Then you do the same with your other arm, while counting from one to eight. Next, kick a leg as if trying to flick mud from the end of your shoe, counting to eight, and repeat with the other leg. Now count to six for each arm and leg, then count to four and finally two for each limb, while flicking them about. This should be fast and noisy.

Then get everyone to count to one for each arm and each leg before shouting, "Rubber chicken!" The rubber chicken is a full-on wiggling shake, and everyone has to fling themselves around, making the noise a rubber chicken might make if it were shaken.

Use this whenever you need to stir up the energy and they'll go mad for it.

ONE MINUTE MADNESS

The clue is in the title: One Minute Madness is precisely that. Whether you are at home with the kids or keeping them occupied elsewhere, there are times that quite simply all the planning, all the cleverness, all the experience and all the trickery in the world just doesn't work. Everyone is a bit over-excited, either in a good way or a bad way, and there is nothing for it but one minute of total madness.

For this, have a specific track of music to hand that you can play which is totally and utterly out of control. When the energy gets to that point where nobody can hold on to a shred of sense anymore, it's time for One Minute Madness. When this happens, press play – and the first person to get nowhere wins. Everybody must move everything all at once: every part of the body must be involved. There are no other rules, there is no aim – this is simply one minute of madness.

If you like, you can give away a prize at the end of the week for whoever went the maddest in the One Minute of Madness, but aside from this there should be no structure. You say go, they go! And everyone stops when time's up: one minute of complete lawlessness.

SPHERE OF CHEERS

As most people know, there is nothing nicer than the sound of a round of applause for something you've done. Applause is normally retained for high status occasions, graduations or some sort of performance. But I worked a long time ago with an amazing practitioner called Hannelore, who would do what she called the Sphere of Cheers at the end of every session.

The Sphere of Cheers is a pleasant and loving way to round off play, to remove any tension or even to celebrate time together as a family. An end-of-holiday Sphere of Cheers, for example, would be a great way to round off a trip together. Most families who spend time together on holiday will have experienced a fair bit of friction as well as some happy days. The Sphere of Cheers is a way of culminating the experience in a positive and fun way.

As always, you need to set an example by shamelessly going healthily way over the top! Get everyone together in a circle and, with meaningful eye contact, ask one person at a time to break from the circle and walk around it slowly until they return to their place. While they do this, everyone else claps. The applause is continuous; however, as the person walks past somebody in the circle, that person rotates to face the walker while clapping, cheering and praising them: You're amazing! You're brilliant! Fantastic! Whoop, whoop! There is a general hubbub of applause that follows the walker almost like a Mexican wave around the circle, filling them with positivity.

GAMES TO GET THE ENERGY UP!

If you want to liven things up, here is an electrician's toolbox of games to help you get everyone buzzing again.

GAME 1: RED ROVER

Red Rover, or Breakthrough as it's called in Romania, is one of the most rambunctious and boisterous games, and probably not encouraged in the school playground. However, if you are playing with a trusted group of friends on soft grass, I don't see any reason why you can't have fun with this game.

You will need:
Eight or more participants in two teams
Enough room for players to run between the teams
Force and willpower!

Step 1. Organize your players into two teams: each team lines up side by side and hold hands to create a chain, facing the opposition. There should be a distance of around 7–10m (approx. 23–33ft) between the two lines.

Step 2. Make the challenge: the first team decides who they want to choose from the opposition. Then they challenge that person, saying: "Red rover, red rover, we call [name] over." At this point, the named person runs at the other group and attempts to break through the line of people. As the line is holding hands, it involves brute force and a bit of a struggle to get through. If the named player manages to break through the line, they return to their original team. If they cannot get through, they join the challenging team.

Step 3. Deciding the winner: the team that ends with the most people after a specific time limit, or which takes everybody from the opposition is the winner.

GAME 2: HULA SNAKE ISLAND

Working on a similar premise to Musical Statues, Hula Snake Island is way cooler and a great party game. It's good for breaking down social barriers too: when a bunch of people are sharing a single hula-hoop, they simply have to work together.

You will need:
Six or more players
One hula hoop for every two players taking part
Enough space to spread out the hoops
Accompanying music

Step 1. Spread out the hoops over the floor: there only should be half as many hoops as there are participants, so that players have to share them.

Step 2. Start dancing: when the music plays, everyone dances frenetically around the room – but not inside the hoops.

Step 3. Stop the music: when the music stops, everyone has to jump inside a hoop, even if it means sharing.

Step 4. The snake strikes: the leader of the game raises his or her hand to imitate a snake's head. Anyone who isn't standing safely inside a hoop is now captured by the snake. Then, in a loud hissy voice, the snake tells the players how many hoops they are going to lose and selects that number of hoops to take away. People safely inside in a hoop can try to dissuade the snake from taking their hoop.

Step 5. Play until the snake is sated: the music comes back on and everyone plays on until there is only one hoop left.

GAME 3: ZOMBIE

This is the perfect game to play as a family or with a bunch of children who don't really know each other very well. The irony is that Zombie is a great game for releasing pent-up energy: after all, what's scarier than being chased around by a lumbering member of the walking dead?

You will need:
Eight or more players
Enough room to run away from each other
A good memory, to remember the names of your co-players

Step 1. Everyone says their name: if you don't know each other very well, make a circle and ask everyone to say their name, going round the circle twice, once clockwise and once anti-clockwise.

Step 2. Choose a zombie: the zombie walks quickly around the space, with arms outstretched zombie-style, chasing the other players. If the zombie touches you, you are out of the game and can't return until the next round.

Step 3. Choose another victim: if the zombie heads toward you, you can avert their touch by calling out the name of somebody else in the group. The person whose name you call then becomes the zombie and the original member of the walking dead goes back to being a civilian. The game continues until there are only two people left, who become the champions.

EXCUSES, EXCUSES...

There's no such thing as too much energy. If you think you're putting in enough energy, put in some more. If you feel like that's all the energy you have, dig deeper. You need to somehow find a way to meet the children's energy and raise them one level. When I'm training or working with my team, I will say to them that if the show is one hour long, that hour should be the most energized hour of everyone's lives! At the end of that hour, all the kids taking part should feel exhausted from their fingertips to their toes.

Playing with children is not about, or at least it shouldn't be, managing and curtailing their energy into an adult sphere. They are not adults, nor should they be asked to pretend they are. They don't have to do as an adult would do. Telling someone below the age of 51 to grow up is, I think, is an act of total violence. You have to make them safe, you have to make them feel loved and supported, but you have to encourage them to be who they are. And, for the majority of children, who they are is someone with a lot more energy than they are usually allowed to express. So we bring more, more and more again.

There are a few common mistakes people make when attempting to justify low energy and a lack of commitment to play. One is: "I'm too old, I can't do that anymore." This is possibly the poorest excuse that exists. Energy starts with the heart, shines through your eyes and goes from there. There are people who run marathons right up until their 95th birthday and beyond, because they have a mental commitment to remaining joyful and energized. Obviously physical decline is a fact, but the energy of your heart is not restricted by the age of your body; it is limited only by your attitude.

Another excuse that I sometimes come across is that high energy is synonymous with being loud and that it's not appropriate in certain environments. Again, this is a misconception. Often when I'm training team members, I will say that I need more volume but no more noise: when you raise your energy, you do not have to go faster or go louder; in fact, the biggest challenge sometimes to make yourself appear extremely small, slow and quiet whilst remaining entirely energized. There is something utterly magical about tiptoeing and whispers that can capture an entire auditorium. Energy is not linked to volume; nor is it linked to speed and size. It is linked only to your personal presence and intention to light the fires in the imaginations of who you are with.

The final justification I get is that it is in some way undermining and inappropriate for a person of assumed status (such as a parent or teacher) to be seen to act in a childish way. I would ask all of you to think back to the teachers, practitioners or mentors who influenced you the most when you were younger. (For more on mentors, see Chapter 8.) Personally, I can identify many qualities that I didn't like or respect in adults, but I don't believe playfulness was ever one of them. If anything, I think sharing a sense of humour and warmth probably gave me the confidence to reveal more of myself in response. This doesn't mean we have to be forever joking and devoid of discipline, but playfulness can be a shortcut to good communication with young people in many situations. In this way a mutual respect can form, and there is the possibility for genuine influence and positive impact, both ways.

Once we've put aside some of our own inhibitions and committed our energy to play, the next step is to gain the confidence to play big – knowing that where we lead by example, others will follow without hesitation.

CHAPTER 5

BE BRAVE AND GO BIG

"Childhood is not age specific, it is attitude specific - so get silly!"

As you might have guessed by now, "going big" isn't about imposing our will on kids in order to get them to obey our instructions; going big is about meeting them playfully and confidently on their own terms so that they are willing to work with us on an energetic level. When we gain their trust in this way, we can turn up the volume at times and take things to the max without worrying about the potential consequences.

Many years ago, I was involved in an annual community event that provided entertainment for children in a certain area of London. Many of the kids had a range of challenges which meant they needed extra support in school and at home. It was particularly difficult to engage with one young man, who was extremely energetic and very strong, yet who had a very limited concentration span.

One year later, however, I was amazed to discover the young man seemed to be in a completely different headspace. His mother explained that, with professional support, she had adopted the sensory diet approach. This meant adapting experiences and activities to include his natural instincts and preferences. The example she gave me was bath time: they had waterproofed the entire bathroom so that rather than try to get him to stay still, he was encouraged to explore the sensory benefits of water. After his bath, they created a calm atmosphere ready for bedtime. For this, she had learned massage, and rather than just drying the young man with a towel for the sake of drying him, she now used the opportunity to utilize massage techniques to create a sense of relaxation. Whereas bath time and bedtime had once been a very challenging part of her day, by working with his highs and lows of energy, they had managed to establish a more inclusive and respectful way to carry out their daily tasks.

This approach can be applied to almost any situation in which we are engaging with children – whether at home or in a group. It means adapting to and working with natural peaks and troughs of energy. At the Flying Seagull Project, we use it during our music sessions. We start small, say with handclaps and small percussive instruments, then build up the pace and volume gradually but steadily with larger instruments – prepared to go really big. Then we bring it back down again, before building it back up, so that the session is like the rising and falling of waves against the beach. The waves cannot be told to calm down, but if you're approaching them in the right way, they can be calmed – like a tide that goes out ready for a peaceful end to the session. The group goes big, the group goes small; the group goes loud, the group goes quiet. Any time we allow a group of children to explode their energy, we have to be prepared to go big too. Because if we are as big as them, if not bigger, then they will follow when we go smaller. This form is one of the prime areas of non-verbal communication, as the kids tune into the energy that we share with them. Telling someone to be quiet, or slower, is nowhere near as powerful as allowing them to feel that a quieter moment or a slower moment is necessary.

The following activities are designed to allow you to go BIG. Safe, structured and with space to rise and fall, they allow a full throttle, super-charged, loud as thunder expression of energy, which I think is a beautiful and essential part of childhood.

FUNBOTS AND BOX WARS

There is probably no greater joy on earth than turning the giant cardboard box that the new fridge came in into a robot costume. Cereal boxes become biceps, toilet rolls become goggles! But rather than stop at creating a robot costume in your front room, why not take it a step further? As long as you have a robust costume to wear, why not take your robot to the ultimate test? Welcome to Funbots and Box wars!

This activity falls somewhere between being an exercise in recycling, the creation of a new world order and an absolute wild time throwing boxes at each other. It also helps provide a safe space in which to acknowledge, express and release the reckless, wild and slightly fiery nature that lies within all of us. It's about experiencing a full-body explosion of fun and laughter.

You will need:
A range of boxes: e.g. made from cardboard, recyclable plastic, egg boxes, cereal boxes – you get the idea!
Scissors
PVA glue, glue sticks, parcel tape, sticky tape, etc.
Decorative extras such as tinfoil, coloured paper, water-based paints (available in powder form), felt-tip pens, sequins, wool, whatever you like – as long as it's recyclable
Plenty of space to do battle, such as a garden, a school hall, the recreation ground, anywhere big enough to handle the apocalypse ...
At least two people to take part
Access to recycling bins

Step 1. Gather the materials to build your funbots: from the cardboard to the decorative extras, wherever possible, re-purpose old items and materials. Make sure that everything you use is recyclable as it is going to be thrown away afterwards.

Step 2. Create your funbot: stick together the dismantled boxes to make a wearable and durable funbot suit for each participant, complete with a separate body and headpiece. Include eyeholes and armholes, so that you can move about in it. Decorate it with paints and other extras. Take your time and make it as elaborate as you like.

Step 3. Choose your box wars location wisely: you will need quite a lot of space, where there won't be any risk of a projectile breaking anything accidentally or disturbing anybody who is not taking part in the activity. The arena for your funbot war should be big enough so that you can run, jump and duck out of the way – but, most importantly, it should be a place where you can all go wild. If you are organizing this on a larger scale, perhaps you could speak to a local school and borrow their gymnasium for an afternoon. Make the activity about recycling and any school should be happy to support you.

Step 4. Celebrate your funbot suits: you could have a funbot fashion show or awards ceremony, with prizes for the best hair and biceps, for example! Take loads of photos to commemorate this moment of madness and creativity, and print them out later to put in scrap-books or albums.

Step 5. Decide what form your box war is going to take: is it going to include a game like Capture the Flag, where you tie a piece of fabric on to one of you and the others have to try to capture it? Or maybe a version of Pin the Tail on the Donkey, but instead tape the tail on the bot butt? Or are you going to chuck empty cartons at each other? Whatever the battle, it should have the energy of a snowball fight (but without the wetness, which would make the boxes unrecyclable). Set the parameters and, if you like, establish a sound to start and finish the box war, such as ringing a bell or blowing a whistle. I've said it before, and I'll say it again: make sure that absolutely everybody involved – adults, children, teachers, parents – joins in. As the role models, heroes and mentors of children, it's important that any adults show them how to join in with wholehearted enthusiasm and a broad smile.

Step 6. Recycle the remains: if your funbot suits survive the battle and live to fight another day, great! If not, simply dispose of the pieces in recycling bins.

GOING BIG TO OVERCOME BLOCKS

Besides giving kids the scope to play big, loud and fast, Real Play is often born out of a moment when an idea is forced to come into existence. A moment where a child at first draws a blank, perhaps stutters and hesitates. It is in these moments that – rather than give them options, or feed them words – it is better to look them in the eye, and wait and wait and wait.

Having worked with children who have not been allowed to be independent in their creativity or in their ideas, I've noticed that when you ask them to do something they often don't know how and will look to you for cues. An example of this happened in Romania, where the Flying Seagull Project was running a rural outreach programme. One day I asked the children to draw anything they liked, which we were going to decorate with different sorts of fabrics and textiles, glues and glitter. I hadn't really considered the picture to be any more than a starting point for the rest of the workshop.

Nothing happened. I waited for 15 seconds before asking them again what they wanted to draw. In reply, they asked what I wanted them to draw. I made the mistake of naming items, not meaning to feed them any ideas but simply to suggest that they had choices. I mentioned a house and a hot air balloon. Quite quickly the children began to draw, and I felt sure that they had managed to get through that breakthrough moment and find an idea or unlock an image that they held in their head or heart. However, after a few minutes, as I walked around the room, I saw that all of them without exception had drawn either a house or – yes, you guessed it – a balloon.

Breakthrough moments might be uncomfortable at first, but they are as much about overcoming a crisis of confidence and self-belief as they are about navigating some sort of creative block. To make things a whole lot simpler and less stressful, I would suggest helping kids to open up by encouraging a more reckless and uninhibited approach to self-expression through a simple game like the One-Word Yelling Story.

THE ONE-WORD YELLING STORY

Now I'm sure most of you have played a game where you've helped tell a story as part of a group with each person adding one word at a time. Children all over the world love this type of game as you can end up with some very funny stories. This particular version is louder and faster – and a great way of helping anyone who might be feeling a bit blocked, or have a reason to hold back, to engage without becoming too focused on the content or narrative.

Step 1. Stand in a circle and warm-up: start by playing a response game such as Rubber Chicken (see page 80) to get everyone in the shared silly zone, free of inhibitions and embarrassment.

Step 2. Explain how the One-Word Yelling Story works: standing in the middle of the circle, you will be pointing at each person in turn and they will yell out whatever word pops into their head. Encourage them to speak first and think later; there's no need to be clever. It doesn't even matter if it's even a real word as long as they join in.

Step 3. Get pointing: to make it even more theatrical, use something like a magic wand or a conductor's baton if you like, and push in a playful way for a really fast pace, faster than anybody could possibly tell a decent normal story.

Step 4. Mix it up: start to leap randomly from one person to the other around the circle so that nobody can be sure when it's their turn next. The sense of anarchy creates even more excitement.

Step 5. Let the others have a go at conducting the chaos: within two or three turns, hand over the baton either literally or metaphorically and substitute yourself with somebody else.

Besides being fun, the purpose of this game is not to make the story cohesive; the purpose is to break down the barriers of restriction that are placed on us when we worry about being good enough rather than throwing ourselves into play and having fun.

Reward Bravery

Any time you ask somebody to reveal themselves, any time you encourage an inhibition to fall away, any time you put a person – young or old – on the spot and create a sense of tension, you must support it and hold that person with the greatest energy you can muster. Actively be there for them; never let them drown in embarrassment. That is how you will create an atmosphere of safety and nurture trust, and that is how you will safely liberate the fire from within them.

CACOPHONY ORCHESTRA

The purpose of cacophony orchestra is to reconnect with the fun of reckless and over-the-top noisemaking. Once children start school, very often their musical interactions begin to take on a more structured form; for example, they might start learning an instrument and musical notation. This is fantastic and in no way would I suggest that encouraging the learning of an instrument is anything other than a wonderful idea, if that's what your children would like to do. But this game is about rekindling the natural connection that we intuitively feel with music, which can be lost during the course of childhood. It's a particularly good game to play once you have done "The One-Word Yelling Story" and will bring in even more energy.

You will need:
Two or more participants
A collection of defunct or homemade, improvised instruments, such as a violin without strings that can be used as a drum, paper-plate tambourines with stuck-on bells, a pot filled with beads to rattle or a rubber chicken that when squeezed makes a funny sound

Step 1. Choose the lead character of an imaginary film: the premise of Cacophony Orchestra is that collectively you are going to create the music for a film that doesn't exist, and which no-one will ever see or hear, but is still exciting. Start by asking everyone what the film is about or, more importantly, who or what. Establish details such as where this person, creature or thing lives, what the character's name is and what time of year the story takes place.

Step 2. Plan a film treatment: once you have these basic details, collectively decide what's going to happen in the film, in terms of a crisis. (Explain that all films have a crisis moment that then finds a resolution.) An example of one of our stories from the past was about a pig called Colin who couldn't find any bread to make a sandwich and was in love with a flamingo. It can be as ridiculous as that; as in any game, the purpose is not the end result but the process.

Step 3. Refine the plot: fine-tune the story so that it has at least six or seven over-the-top points where you can bring in an orchestra to mark the different emotional highlights, explaining the dynamic of each of these scenes. These ridiculous scenarios are going to be accompanied by an equally outrageous cacophony. For example, a rubber chicken solo might accompany a love scene whereas the score for a battle scene might include a rousing rattle and drum beat.

Step 4. Equip your orchestra and start the score: making sure everybody has an instrument or two to play, narrate the story and signal for them to come in at the key moments. The trick is to keep it well paced. This game is not meant to last for very long, but it's a fantastic way to rekindle children's enthusiasm for music and group play.

PUBLIC PLAY

In *A Return to Love*, spiritual activist Marianne Williamson states: "It is our light, not our darkness that most frightens us. We ask ourselves, 'Who am I to be brilliant, gorgeous, talented, and fabulous?' Actually, who are you not to be?" This attitude can be very handy when facing shyness or embarrassment about playing big. Going big and getting radical means facing our own inhibitions, as well as supporting children as they face theirs. And it is nothing less than our duty to those who look to us for encouragement.

I'm not suggesting every parent-figure or teacher behaves like a loud and brash clown, but, as we've seen, there does need to be a willingness to go big and shine as a tool to show others that it's okay for them to do so too. This is especially important when we are interacting with those who are perhaps in some way different to mainstream society, as they will be acutely aware of their sense of separation from others and perhaps have a greater struggle to find a platform from which to express themselves. This is why I advocate a sort of "making a fool of yourself" approach – not only because it's more fun, but because it serves a much higher purpose.

If we make light of personal flaws, and play with social awkwardness and inhibition, we lessen the hold of these on everyone else. So the next two exercises are purposefully ludicrous, meaningfully embarrassing and consciously uncomfortable for the parent or play leader – and they are to be tried out publicly. That way, you can face your critics and show your kids that eccentricity and uniqueness are something to celebrate. Finally, three words of advice: get over yourself!

MAKE A LOUD NOISE NOW!

Most of us are completely unprepared to do in public what we would willingly do in the privacy of our own homes or even in the classroom. The very idea of people seeing us seems like one of the most terrifying prospects there is. Yet going big in public, and demystifying the threat of the judgement of strangers, are massive parts in liberating play and liberating innovation through play. To help shed your own inhibitions, quite simply make a loud noise right now! Whoever you are with, flip a coin so that one person becomes the caller and another the noisemaker. At any point, anywhere, the caller can tell the noisemaker to make a great, big, unashamedly loud noise, and the person who has lost the coin flip has to do precisely that, wherever they are!

REAL-LIFE REMOTE CONTROL

You are going to make a real-life remote control. One person is going to use it (and, who knows, they might become a famous TV producer as a result), while the other person is going to be controlled by it. At the very least, you will have a lot of fun and create positive memories to look back on.

You will need:
A narrow cardboard box (e.g. a tissue box)
A permanent marker pen
Glue and scissors (optional)
Black paint (optional)
Tinfoil (optional)

Step 1. Create your remote: use the marker pen to draw "buttons" on the box and mark these with their functions: fast-forward, rewind, pause, at least four different channels, and a volume control. If you want a more elaborate remote control, paint the box black and create buttons from circles of the tinfoil.

Step 2. Choose who gets to use it first: flip a coin to see who goes first as the remote-control operator and who is controlled by the TV remote.

Step 3. Press play: practise in the house or classroom, then try using the control in public. The controller presses the button and tells the person being controlled what they've pressed. When they press fast-forward you know what to do ... The bigger and sillier and more exaggerated your actions, the better. If there are a few of you, you could split up into groups with a control each.

GAMES TO BRING OUT THE BIG!

When you want to pump up the volume and encourage kids to play big, here are some great games to bring out boldness.

GAME 1: THE CIRCLE OF BOOM!

This game is about speed, precision and concentration. But it's also highly loud and theatrical, with an old-fashioned Wild West theme. After the first couple of times that you've played it, it's a game that anybody can lead.

You will need:
Seven or more participants
Enough space to stand shoulder to shoulder in a circle
To be the quickest draw in the West!

Step 1. Stand in the middle of the circle and explain the rules: when you point at somebody in the circle, that person has to crouch down very quickly. Then the two people on either side must draw their pistols (i.e. their fingers and thumb in the shape of a gun) and quickly fire at each other, shouting, "BOOM!" The first person to shout BOOM while pointing their fingers will survive; the person who draws second is out.

Step 2. Introduce some theatre to make losing fun: encourage them to die in over-the-top and dramatic ways. Whoever is out, stays sitting "dead" on the floor.

Step 3. Continue to the next round: the person who had to crouch down initially now stands back up, and you carry on the game by pointing randomly at someone else in the circle. When there is a gap because somebody is out, the shooters have to take aim at the next person along – later in the game, and depending on the numbers of players, this could be as many as three or four people away.

Step 4. Time for the final showdown: once you are down to only two players, they should stand back to back like duellists and – slowly counting from one to ten – take a step away on each number. When you shout, "Ten!" they draw, turn and shout BOOM! in an old Wild West-style showdown. The fastest gun wins.

GAME 2: FOOT-PAINT DANCING

Foot-paint dancing is one of my all-time favourite things to do. It's a great activity to follow another musical game such as Musical Statues, and combines at least two different types of expression – art and music – but without getting hung up on the results.

You will need:

A long roll of scrap wallpaper (plain if possible), which can be second-hand – it should have a non-plastic surface

Water-based paints, which have been mixed to a thick consistency, or poster paints

Three deep-sided trays that are large enough to put a foot in (old oven trays are fine)

Two old towels

Washing-up bowl with warm water and soap

Lively music to accompany foot-paint dancing (protect the music system in plastic if necessary)

Gaffer tape

Plastic groundsheet or a floor that can be mopped clean afterwards

Step 1. Set up: lay the wallpaper on the floor in a strip that is approx. 5m long (or 15ft). Secure it in place with gaffer tape at the corners and at 2m (7ft) intervals along the course. Pour the paint into the trays, with a little bit on the plastic ground sheet at the head of the wallpaper strip. Place a bowl of warm water on the plastic sheeting at the far end, near where the children will come off the paper.

Step 2. Bare those toes: ask everyone to take off their shoes and socks. Feet without socks on can be quite embarrassing for some kids, so it's good to make a game of it. To take the focus off the feet themselves, you could, for example, ask them to draw with a pencil around their soles first.

Step 3. Paint your feet and play that music: so the session doesn't immediately get out of hand, ask the children to dip their feet in the paint one at a time and then ask each dancer to step on the paper and demonstrate a dance style that they prefer, or one they feel would make a good pattern. While the music plays, they are to dance, stomp and sway their way along the paper until they get to the far end.

Step 4. Clean, dry – and repeat: when they reach the far end of the paper, everyone is to clean their feet in the bowl and dry them properly with one of the towels before returning for another go. (Depending on the age of the children, it might be an idea to ask another adult to help you with this foot-cleaning stage and also to make sure they don't slip over on the wet paper.)

Step 5. Dance in rounds: turn off the music after each round of dancing and start again with another track in a different style or rhythm, replacing the paper as often as you like. Encourage experimentation, such as two people dancing at the same time or different colours on different feet. After about half an hour, stop dancing.

Step 6. Take your creations on to the next stage: at the end, you might have a lot of non-usable pieces of dripping-wet, paint-covered paper, or some beautiful pieces of art. The result is totally irrelevant, but if you wish, you can use the paper to make something else, such as a mural of giant feet cut out of the painted wallpaper – or whatever else you like!

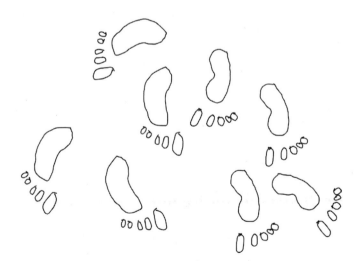

GAME 3: BULLDOG

Bulldog is a fantastic game for getting the energy up to the max, taking risks and playing big. As long as it's properly introduced, it's not as risky as some people believe.

You will need:
Eight or more players
Enough space to run between two points, which is free of obstacles and has soft ground (e.g. a clearly defined area on a playing field)
Speed, agility, determination

Step 1. Choose one person to be the bulldog: the bulldog is going to stand guard in the middle of the run zone and try to catch runners. In order to capture them, the bulldog has to grab them and hold on long enough to shout, "Bulldog one, two, three!"

Step 2. The rest of the participants have to avoid capture: the runners have to make it safely from one side of the danger zone all the way across to the other side.

Step 3. The bulldog wins team-mates: once a runner has been caught by the bulldog, he or she then joins the bulldog and the pair of you face the runners once again. By the end of the game, there should only be one or two runners left.

Step 4. Keep the rounds clear: in order to keep this game ordered and regulated, ask the bulldog(s) to give you a woof-woof or wolf's howl, and the runners to shout "Mamma Mia!" in their loudest voices before each run. That way, the structure and pace of the game can be monitored by you.

THE BEAUTY OF GOING BIG

One striking memory of being brave and going big comes from a time when I was working in Romania in a school for children with special needs. Having arrived in the morning expecting a group of maybe five or ten children, the groups numbered around 50, the majority of whom had Down syndrome and who were able-bodied and very excited to be taking part in something new and unusual. When the children were encouraged to go bigger by me, making noise with musical instruments, they were amazed that they were allowed to do so; which meant that when I decided to go quieter, they were happy to follow my example. I had acknowledged what they wanted and willingly given them permission to push the boundaries. This gave me the right to lead, and they were happy following, so that when I went quiet they did too – much to the astonishment of the school's staff.

What normally holds people back with children, especially those with learning difficulties, is the fear of going too far or overstimulation. This is a very real fear, but it's something we have to master rather than shy away from. All children have the innate desire to shout and clap and dance and make noise. Rather than try to contain that vibrant energy, or control it, I would rather divert it and – to use the diet metaphor – feed it into a regime that allows moments of chocolate, let's call it, mixed with pieces of fruit, and of course a nice healthy sandwich.

Have confidence that you can lead – and then lead. Lead children into full self-expression, loud and soft, big and small, and you will leave them content that they have proclaimed their personality to the stars above. You will also allow them to let their creativity shine, which leads us neatly on to Chapter 6.

CHAPTER 6

CREATIVITY NEEDS YOU!

"Within the world of creativity there's no such thing as wrong!"

When people talk about creativity, often they mean the arts and those individuals who paint, write or perform. I believe that creativity is really far broader than that sort of definition, and can be applied to all areas of life, including science, inventions and social innovations. Creativity is about imagining a different way of doing things, and, when accompanied by self-belief, it can completely change the world.

At the heart of creativity lies the imagination, a key to understanding our past, recognizing our present and building our future. Anybody who is familiar with the work of the author and educationalist Ken Robinson will already know this theory: that if you teach a child innovation and confidence in their ideas and who they are, and if you encourage them to create new things, when they eventually enter society in any field – be it the civil service, medicine, politics, refuse collection, teaching or whatever – they will have the tools they need to adapt and flourish in the years to come. If we merely teach them the techniques and methods that apply to how we live now, we teach them concepts that will be obsolete by the time they reach the workplace.

Most importantly, if we are going to benefit our global community and tackle its many problems, we desperately need to teach our children to imagine, create and innovate. We must give them the confidence and encouragement to believe that they can make a difference to the world. And we can do this through Real Play, showing them how to have faith in and be proactive in their creativity. We can show them how to turn their ideas into reality, using a strategy that means those ideas won't disappear into nothingness, or develop in ineffective ways. For this, we can use the "INDEED" process:

- **I**magination: engaging the imagination in response to the world.
- **N**eed: identifying a particular situation that we want to address.
- **D**ecision: making definite decisions in response to that situation.
- **E**nergy: putting a serious amount of ENERGY into making our idea work.
- **E**motional commitment: bringing passion to it, in order to realize an idea to its fullest extent.
- **D**etermination: refusing to take "no" for an answer and chasing our dream as if there is no other option.

The good news is that, with children, tapping into creativity is like drawing water from the deepest well that ever existed. This is because children still instinctively explore the world through their imaginations. As parents, teachers and play leaders, our job is to figure out structured yet unconventional and therefore engaging ways to direct that creativity and energy without trampling on their freedom.

In this chapter, we will be looking at some activities that create a particular platform and environment for creativity to express itself. While this book includes many other activities that do this, the focus here is on that special creative crunch-moment – when there is nothing else to fall back on, and we have to look inside ourselves to find the word when no other word exists; where we freeze, stutter and stumble just before bringing something new into being where once there was nothing. This is the moment of inspiration, and we have to teach our children to recognize it, and to break through it with gusto, excited to explore what lies beyond.

This doesn't mean that we have to follow through on every single idea; of course not: if you were to ask the average seven-year-old for a list of ten inventions, at least nine of them would be so utterly ridiculous you probably wouldn't even recognize the picture on the paper. But it means that inhibition and fear become lessened in the process of creativity. At some point, as we've seen, most of us stopped doing something because we no longer felt we were any good at it. The same is true of creativity more generally. We have to remove the notion of success as being the end result of creativity, and place the focus on celebrating the actual process of creating something, no matter how ludicrous it may be. If creativity only engages a technical approach then it is nothing. It should involve these three Ps: personality, principles and purpose.

By engaging children in exercises and games using the Real Play approach, I believe we can help to reduce the impact of rising inhibitions in their early years and early teens, and instead begin to build a clear path to guide them through those moments where they might trip and falter on the obstacles of doubt. By ensuring that we include Real Play essentials such as humour in activities to remove the pressure of perfection, and the choose-to-lose technique so that winning is only one of the options to consider when embarking on a project, we can protect them against internalizing the failing elements of any creative process.

Instead, we show how failure means that we get to try again and create something new, and thus it should always be an element that we celebrate. We might have to do something wrong a hundred times before we begin to get it right. It is our responsibility as parents, play leaders, rabble-rousers and teachers to lessen the impact of, and to help children move beyond, the fear of failure, the fear of looking foolish, and the fear of no-one listening. We must help them to discover their own strengths, invent and hone their ideas, and teach them to use these tools to go on and change the world. I truly believe that it is creativity that will save us – and this planet on which we reside.

HOMEMADE TV

Okay, so this might sound rather controversial, but I'm just going to come right out and say it: most TV is rubbish – poorly executed, boringly passive and irritatingly repetitive. While I won't refute there is a place for a television in every household, it's in the loft in a box with "do not open" written on it. I propose a radical change to the way we spend our evenings, and this begins with a campaign against mindless television watching. To make this move slightly more bearable, however, I have come up with an alternative: homemade TV!

You will need:
Cardboard and glue (optional)
Additional homemade props (optional)
A sense of humour
Will power

Step 1. Remove the TV from your front room: boot-sale it, donate it to charity, hide it or give it to a friend or, better, somebody you don't really like.
Step 2. Make your own TV space: this can either be a TV screen made from cardboard, or a particular space in your front room to act as your new focal point. It should be large enough to fit two fully grown humans. This will be your modern television theatre.

Step 3. Come up with your own original TV shows: take a bit of time to write and rehearse your homemade TV shows. Maybe spend an hour or so on this at first, although once you immerse yourself in the process, you might find it takes over your weekends. Aim for a varied programme, maybe with a family show, some stand-up comedy or reality TV, depending on everyone's tastes. The nightly news is quite fun as it can become a great way of sharing your day with each other: "Family news at six – Dad had a bad day because he forgot his lunch!"

Step 4. Create some props: if you wish, with a little help, add a few extras such as a Hollywood-style clapperboard or an autocue (if you can be bothered to write everything out). You could even make lists for the final credits, naming anyone who takes part in your shows, including the writer, director, sound effects and costume, etc. If you like, build, buy or borrow props and costumes.

Step 5. Rehearse if you wish: however, if you do choose to rehearse your show, the rehearsal process could be extremely informal and almost pointlessly daft.

Step 6. Make Homemade TV night part of your household routine: I would recommend enjoying Homemade TV at least once a month. Make it something that everybody can take part in, with each person choosing how to express him- or herself individually. There will definitely be some reluctance to join in at first, and this is okay too, but after the first fun family TV night, there will be a more eager participatory vibe.

Step 7. Hold your own FTV Awards ceremony: as an added extra, at the end of the year or summer, hold your own Family TV Awards night. The awards can be for things like the silliest costume, shortest show and least interesting piece of news – whatever you like on this party occasion. Sometimes these awards nights can end up being more fun than the TV shows themselves, but the main thing is to create a way to interact that doesn't have the numbing of a passive night in front of the TV. You could even schedule your own Christmas special for

those who can't be with you; film it and send it to family and friends – a winter warmer if ever there was one.

Having said all that, a Saturday night with dinner on your lap, wrapped in blankets or sipping a hot chocolate with the family – all watching mindless TV – can also be pretty relaxing from time to time, so maybe don't throw out the TV quite yet ...

THE INVISIBLE BOX OF EVERYTHING

I've played this game on every continent, with groups who have everything and those who literally don't even have a roof over their heads. Time and again, it's become clear to me that the truest riches in this life are born of our imaginations. This game is intended to create a feeling of wealth beyond measure, and it's about conjuring up something out of nothing. The final thing to say before we get stuck in, is never underestimate the draw of the Invisible Box of Everything; I have knelt in the mud of the toughest slums in West Africa with teenage boys known for their toughness and seen them desperate for their turn to open the lid, exclaim "Oh *là là*" and share their imaginations with the world!

Step 1. Create a circle: wait until everyone has expended a bit of energy before gathering them together. Then, with a wide-eyed expression on your face, say, "Wow!" because you've glimpsed an incredible sight behind one of them. Make your way over and mime picking up a heavy cardboard box. Then present your invisible square box to the circle, placing it carefully in the middle.

Step 2. Open the box: mime undoing a latch, then open the lid and glance down inside the invisible box. What you see is amazing and you exclaim, "Oh là là!" With gestures and facial expressions, encourage everyone to repeat "Oh là là!" after you.

Step 3. Unpack the box: begin by pulling out a simple item and share it with everyone. This could an imaginary bicycle, a fishing rod, a basketball; something that is easily identifiable and which will be understood by the group using even the most basic mime skills. Hand this item to somebody in the circle, such as another adult, who understands what is happening and can help you demonstrate what the game entails.

Step 4. Encourage everyone to have a go: each player chooses the next participant to unpack the box, making sure that everybody takes a turn, even if they look uncertain, intimidated or shy. Using strong eye contact and enthusiasm to offer them support, don't give them suggestions, but let them meet that uncomfortable brick wall that forces creation. All they need to know is that inside this empty box is everything that has ever existed, that could ever exist, and even some other things too. It could be something such as a zombie, or a wild dog. Whatever you can imagine, whatever you can name, it's already inside the box...

The purpose of the game is for the participants to meet a challenge and, with the support of everyone else, to manage to push their way through it, and receive the praise for having done so. It doesn't matter what they pull out of the box: every single thing is the right thing and the winning choice. There is absolutely no such thing as "wrong" in a game where you're pulling something non-existent from an imaginary box and showing it to people who cannot see it. Perfect.

MEETING THE CHALLENGE OF DISCOVERY

One of the most important parts of leading play, whether it be in your home or in your place of work, is to help kids make their way through the challenge of discovery: to break through that moment where they don't yet know the answer and to find a response. Though this may seem slightly dramatic when we're simply talking about children's games, the habit of meeting challenges with confidence and positivity, or otherwise, is formed in the early years of childhood.

A negative or pessimistic parent or teacher can have an impact that, at the time, might seem insignificant but with the fertilization of the years can lead to some very uncomfortable and unhappy adults. In many ways (and as will become clear in Chapter 7), the purpose of play is to meet challenges in a safe and supportive environment so that we can learn that challenges are something we can get through; and that we are good enough and valuable enough and can make it safely through the other side.

TAKE EVERYTHING OUT – PUT IT ALL BACK AGAIN!

This game can make you feel like your brain is a balloon about to pop, but it's a perfect way to get people to think at the speed necessary to create and to imagine. It's also a great exercise to do at the beginning of a play session, as it forces everyone to be completely in the moment, and leave behind whatever they might have had in their heads before they started playing. Like the Invisible Box of Everything, it doesn't rely on any props – just pure imagination.

Step 1. Open the imaginary cupboard: explain that you need everybody's help to empty a large cupboard which holds everything that has ever existed or has ever been thought of. It all has to come out of the cupboard immediately!

Step 2. Get everyone emptying: your role as a chaos instigator is to push them to go faster and faster. They should be pulling out everything from giraffes to sandwiches to roller skates to roast dinners to aeroplanes to members of their own family. Let this run for at least 30 seconds to a minute, until people are yelling absolute twaddle as they reach into the creative parts of their brain.

Step 3. Get them to put everything back: without warning, tell everyone that they have been extremely badly behaved by emptying the cupboard – and that everything they have thrown on the floor needs to be tidied away immediately. Here's the twist: in the same order it came out. (This is obviously impossible, but it'll get that lovely reaction of a giggle crossed with a groan.) Before they have a chance to think, get them started and push them faster and faster!

This is a game that can be played over and over again, even in the car if you are getting bored of the music choice. For kids who are living in difficult situations, or if there's been any tension in the room, such as sibling rivalry, it's a great way to reset the scales, ready for a play session that doesn't hang on to those troubles.

THIS IS YOUR LIFE

This game is a real test of creativity and imagination. It's also a sign that you're getting old, if, like me, you recognize the name of the TV show! For those of you who don't known it, *This is Your Life* was a programme in which an unsuspecting minor celebrity would be invited to an event, such as a book signing or awards ceremony, only to find that the whole thing was a set-up. Instead, they would be presented with a large red book by the TV host and told, with an appropriately over-the-top theme song, "Thiiiiiiiis is your liiiiiiiiiiiife!" Then it would be back to the studio, where the person would meet individuals who had once featured in their life in some way – from, say, a favourite teacher to their first boss. It was always a big surprise as they usually hadn't seen each other for a long time.

This live version is performed on the spot and can be played anywhere: it's perfect in the car, if there is wet weather and you can't go out, at sleepovers or just as fun after dinner when you're relaxing in the lounge. In this version, simply pick somebody and start fabricating an entire imaginary history for them, such as choosing someone who is seven or eight years old – and then talking about their early years growing up in northern Canada in 1925. The more elaborate and the sillier you can be, the funnier and more ridiculous this game becomes.

To make it like the show, call on members of the "audience" to become key featured people. So, for example, you might say, "Do you remember your maths teacher, Mr Wrigglesworth, and that famous catchphrase of his? Well he's here tonight ..." At which point you gesture to somebody in the group who has to jump up and join the improvisation by pretending to be Mr Wrigglesworth and knowing already that famous phrase of his. Keep supporting anyone through hesitations and blanks. Just to remind you, you will also of course have to take your turn!

CREATIVE CAR RIDES

Whether we like it or not, most of us will inevitably end up spending a large amount of time stuck in the car as a family, either going to Grandma's house, during the school run or setting out on holiday. When I was younger, we used to play a mixture of "I Spy", "I went to the market...", and "Keep quiet in the back – apparently the maps are wrong and your dad's lost again!" Well, with the invention of GPS, getting lost is no longer such an issue, which in some ways is a bit of a shame. (My dad used to say a car journey wasn't a car journey until you got a bit of grass stuck between the wheels.)

Either way, maps are now sorted, so there's a lot more possibility in the car for creative interaction and play – instead of simply handing the kids a tablet computer with Minecraft or some other such dirge on it, and allowing the hypnotic and mildly addictive nature of such games to keep them quiet the entire journey.

Here are four quick games for the car.

GAME 1: HIDE THE SHOE

In this game, the person whose turn it is gets to "hide the shoe" anywhere in history – past, present or future – and within fact or fiction, or somewhere totally abstract. They say, "I've hidden the shoe", while clearly picturing where that shoe is. Then everyone else in the car has to ask them questions with a "yes" or "no" answer. Sometimes it can be easy to find the shoe: it might be hidden, for instance, in the washing machine at Granny's house, or in Mum's wardrobe. But the more you play, the more outrageous and peculiar it can get. For example, one of my friends adopted this game for their car journeys, and their little boy Henry hid the shoe between the number 1 and

the 3 in the number 13. Another time the shoe was hidden on Gandalf's foot as he said, "You shall not pass!" in *The Lord of the Rings* movie. So you see, this game bends time, space, reality – and everything else besides.

GAME 2: COLLECTIVE SUPERHERO

Taking it in turns, going round the car, you collectively invent a new superhero. Do this by adding one word each to the description. So, for example, the game could go like this: "The ... name ... of ... this ... superhero ... is ... Lawnmower ... Juggler ... Girl ... Cat!" Each person, being allowed only one word, will no doubt try to project their opinion or idea onto the superhero. Once you have a name, describe your superhero's costume, superpowers and weaknesses. It can be really funny hearing everyone's ideas – and there's no pressure, because once you have created your superhero, you will no doubt forget about him or her by the time you get out of the car.

GAME 3: "WHEN I'M PRIME MINISTER..."

This works in a similar way to the traditional game "I went to the market ...", when you list the items you would buy, with each player having to remember everything on the growing list. Instead, one of you says, "When I'm prime minister ..." and you describe the new policy you would introduce. The next person then says, "When I'm prime minister ..." and repeats your policy before adding their own to it. You keep going until you have established the profile of a new prime minister or president to take over the safeguarding of your country. Now this will be interesting because the younger generation often has a far better grasp on the political world than those before them did, and will probably have some surprising ideas on policy. When I played this game as a child, our policies would have been about things like introducing chocolate bars for school dinner. Recently, I had an in-depth conversation with one of my nieces about single-use plastics and the environment – and she is only eight!

GAME 4: ANIMAL NAME CHANGE

Every time you see an animal from the beginning of your journey to the end, win a point by being the first to shout out the name of the animal, followed by "I win!" For example: "Cow, I win!"

The creative part comes in the second part, which is to rename your animal with the funniest new name. At this point, everyone in the car has 30 seconds to make up a new name for the creature. So using the example of "Cow, I win", part two might be "splotchy grass muncher", "four-legged milk beast" or "round, soggy pooper". You then decide as a car by voting whose was the funniest and that person gets a point.

The rules are that nobody is allowed to name that animal again during the same car journey, and the next time you play, if somebody remembers that the new name has been used before or something remarkably close to it, it is discounted – but the person does get to try again.

GAMES TO GET CREATIVE

Here's a pack of high-octane games to take the players out of their minds and into their bodies, breaking the hold of their thoughts and freeing the flow of energy. Why not use your imagination and make your own versions of them too?

GAME 1: GO STOP - AND REWIRE YOUR BRAIN

As the name suggests, this is a game aimed at muddling up our brains and rewiring some of our more fixed ideas. This is essentially what creativity is all about: it's about putting different elements together and re-imagining them in a unique way.

You will need:
Three or more players
Enough space so that everybody can walk around without bumping into each other.

Step 1. Explain the rules: when you say "go", everyone has to move around the space; when you say "stop", they have to stop. Say "go", then ask them to go a bit faster – but no running, then get them to stop. Do this a few times until everybody is engaged.
Step 2. Announce it is "time to rewire your brain": (I recommend saying this in the style of an over-the-top American film trailer.) Explain that now when you say "go", you actually mean "stop", and when you say "stop", you really mean "go". In a loud voice, shout, "Go!" Many of them will take a couple of stumbled steps, which you greet with a head shake and a weary, "Now, now, now!" Next, get them moving by shouting "Stop!" A decent bit of teasing here and there will encourage them to giggle at their mistakes rather than feel bad. Play a couple of rounds before moving on to the next stage.
Step 3. Add more instructions: tell them that when you say "jump", everyone should jump in the air, and when you say "clap", they are to clap three times. Try these two new instructions out a couple of times while standing still, then get them moving by yelling "stop" (of course). Try out each of the new commands while they are on the go, then bring them to a standstill by shouting "go". Explain that it is time again to "rewire your brain": when you say "jump", they are to clap; when you say "clap", you mean "jump". Don't be tempted to make it too easy by yelling the command slowly. However, you can help them when you call the word by showing them yourself what you want them to do.

Step 4. Introduce the final layer of commands: for these, I normally use "kick" as if they're scoring a goal, whilst yelling "yeah!" And "punch" whilst punching the air and shouting "whoa!" Follow the same format by introducing the commands the right way round and getting them used to them, before switching them over. Now "go" means "stop" and "stop" means "go"; "clap" means "jump" and "jump" means "clap"; "kick" means "punch" and "punch" means "kick". It's quite fun to sum up by allowing these guys to finish your sentences; for instance, you say, "Stop means...?" And they shout, "Go!" The end of this round should be extremely fast and extremely silly, with everybody feeling completely muddled – as if their brains have been tickled from the inside out.

GAME 2: CAT AND MOUSE IN THE GRID

There is an unavoidable amount of faffery to get this game organized, but once it is up and running, it's one of my all-time favourites.

You will need:
18 or more players (an even number)
Enough space to stand in a square
A lot of patience
A whistle (optional)
Music (optional)

Step 1. Create a grid of players, with two left over: line everyone up in a rectangle or square; so if, say, there are 18 players, the grid would consist of four lines of four people (plus two people left over to play the cat and mouse). The people in the grid should stand an arm's length away from each other. When they face forward with their arms outstretched, they create the walls of four corridors. Make it very clear that their arms are as solid as a brick wall, which cannot be run either through, over or under. When you shout "Switch!" the entire grid is to turn to their right and face in that direction with their arms still outstretched. This will redirect the direction of the corridors.

Step 2. Start the game of chase: the final two players are the cat and the mouse, who start in opposite corners of the grid. The challenge is simply for the cat to catch the mouse. However, you will be calling the game, and when you shout "Switch!" (or blow your whistle), the direction of the corridors will change: though the cat might be just one arm's length away from little mousey, they are instantly cut off by a newly appeared wall. (As with most games, I find this far more enjoyable when there is some encouraging music to quicken the pace.)

Step 3. Refresh your cat and mice: play the game for as long as you like and make it as easy or hard for the cat as you choose by deciding when to call "Switch!" Once the cat has caught the mouse or time has run out, simply ask the cat and mouse to swap places with somebody else in the grid. If you have a mixed group, you can keep it varied by saying the cat has to swap with someone who is taller than they are, or the mouse must find somebody with red shoes, etc. In this way, you can ensure that everybody gets a turn and the cats and mice don't stay within one friendship circle. If you have adults and children playing together, there are few things funnier than a tiny cat chasing an adult-sized mouse.

GAME 3: SHOE GAME
This is a game that makes everyone think on their feet!

You will need:
A caller
Eight or more players to form two teams
Enough space to run between the two teams
A shoe or boot

Step 1. Divide people into two teams of five or more players: the teams form two facing lines approximately 10m (33ft) apart. Place the shoe in the middle of the space between the two lines.

Step 2. Secretly number the team's players: each team must secretly number their players from 1 upward, according to however many people are playing.

Step 3. The caller shouts out a number: now, the corresponding players for that number have to try to do one of two things:

A. Capture the shoe and return it to their line. This results in the return to play of any of the players from that team who have been temporarily kicked out, and the opposing member of the other team being temporarily out.

B. Intercept the opposing player before they can get the shoe safely back to their line. If they are able to touch any part of the player holding the shoe, then that player is then out. (But unlike option A, nobody from their own team returns to play.)

There is an added complication: if you touch the shoe at all, you are committed to return it to your line. This means that if you make a grab at it, but fail to secure it, the opposing team player can tag you at that point – and you will be out. However, throwing the shoe in the air, as long as you catch it before it touches the ground, is permitted.

Step 4. The teams must secretly re-number: once somebody leaves the game (albeit temporarily), the team with the smallest number of players must re-number themselves, including doubling up the digits where necessary to match the number of players on the other side. So, for example, if one team has six players, a team with three players would take on two numbers each. The winning team either has the most players at the end of an allotted time, or wipes out the other team first.

PRAISE CREATIVITY AS MUCH AS CLEVERNESS OR SPORTINESS!

One of the things I've noticed, both from my own upbringing and since I've been working with children, is that we don't often hear the phrase, "Well done, that was so creative!" Now, I know many of you are probably thinking, "But I'm always saying that to my kids", so maybe I'm completely wrong. But what I remember hearing are phrases such as "what a clever boy" or "she's made the football team"; great things, of course – but I think we can all agree that traditionally sport and academia have had a much more prominent place than creativity in terms of what we steer our children toward.

Here, I'm talking about the act of being creative. Children are sometimes subconsciously given negative messages about creativity, such as "don't play with your food" or "stop messing around", yet playing with the world around us and messing about can actually lead to very important output. I'm not suggesting you encourage your children to make sausage-and-mash castles rather than eat their dinner (I know how difficult it is to get children to eat), but when they do something creative, even if it's messy or poorly timed, I would encourage you to praise that creativity – simply for its being creative. It's important to recognize and praise creativity as part of everyday life outside of a structured or assessment-based syllabus.

One of the most endearing and heart-warming things about working with children is when their confidence becomes high enough for them to show the world the absurdities and eccentricities of their personality. And one of the major ways in which they do this is through creative expression. So, as frustrating and befuddling as the behaviour of the children in your family or classroom might be at times, please be careful about how you respond to it: apparent misbehaviour might just be the creative exploration of thoughts and ideas expressed at the wrong moment because of a lack of appropriate time-management skills!

Occasionally kids can go about the right things in the wrong ways, and at those times it's up to us to meet these challenges with as much positivity as we can muster; something which we're going to be looking at next...

CHAPTER 7

MEET CHALLENGE WITH POSITIVITY

"Whatever they said, whatever they did - there's still no such thing as a bad kid."

Whether at home or outside it, children will always present us with moments of intense challenge and conflict. These can be huge or tiny, but all are significant as they represent a genuine form of communication and self-assertion. Defiance is a marker of intense emotion and that's why when children choose to communicate with us through conflict, it is essential to have a plan and the motivation to deal with this sort of challenge as well as we can.

Over the past decade, I have worked with many children who have been extremely challenging, combative, defensive, aggressive and sometimes even violent. There are equally many reasons for this – from the traumatized past of teenagers fleeing warzones, the violence and instability experienced by children in care, those from communities on the very fringes of society, or sometimes simply because a child has not yet found any comfort or direction in life that feels positive and, as such, lives in a state of intense frustration. Whatever the reasons are, what matters is what happens now.

When we are working or playing with children, we need to respond to the needs of children as they present themselves to us in that moment – much as, in Chapter 5, we looked at the benefits of the sensory-diet approach when working with a child's nature, rather than struggling to get the child to conform to a regime that doesn't suit him or her. If, when you've planned a quiet drawing session, you walk in the room to find that the energy is sky-high and extremely chaotic, you need to be ready to adapt.

This doesn't mean that we allow ourselves to be dictated to by children or that we abandon any sort of responsibility to guide them. What it does mean is that we draw upon the experience and inner resources that enable us to be flexible. Similar to how in Chapter 2 we looked at the importance of planning ahead and having a fast version, a slow version and a total abandon-the-game-for-Plan-B option for any activity, we should be prepared to adapt our delivery style, the activity and sometimes even its duration. There is nothing wrong with asking children what they would like to do, especially if it means defusing potential conflict.

There have been many occasions in the refugee camps in Greece, for example, when the weather has affected the work of The Flying Seagull Project. If it's windy or rainy, this can impact dramatically on the ability of the kids to take part in certain activities – and not just in terms of their being physically caught in the rain, but because their psychological state becomes as disordered as the weather. After all, they are only living one thin canvas away from it. In these situations, there is absolutely no point in my trying to run a focused juggling workshop, when it is much more likely that they would prefer to do something more physical. This, in turn, will help them process some of their physical frustrations healthily.

For meaningful play or activity to take place, there absolutely has to be two-way communication and flexibility. If kids respond to your planned activity by saying there is something they would like to do, see where it's possible to compromise. And consider the energy levels of the suggested activity. For example, I don't run football sessions so if they were to turn to me and say, "We want to play football", this wouldn't be something we could agree on. However, by asking for football, they are letting me know that they'd like an activity that's non-cognitive and physical in focus, which means that I can draw on my list of games and activities that meet those criteria.

Equally, there are times when I might ask a group what they would like to do and they will simply say, "Cinema." What they are telling me is that they are physically tired and would like to do something that involves an element of relaxation rather than physical output. If I had planned a football class or a run-around game and they asked for cinema, I would conclude from this that their set of needs is different from that which I came in expecting.

SOCK WRESTLING

As The Flying Seagull Project team has worked with some very volatile communities around the world, we've had to develop ways to allow children to unleash their physical frustrations without anybody getting hurt. With everything going on around them, and all the difficulties of their circumstances, it's obvious that a desire for establishing status or simply fighting back against the injustice will show itself. This will result often in fights and violence. (From my memory of my teenage years at the dreaded Sandy Upper School, to be honest it wasn't much different!)

In many ways, fighting and physical manifestations of frustration are a natural part of childhood, so rather than discrediting or disempowering the culprits, I suggest that where possible we try to redirect this energy so that it can be released safely. This is where sock wrestling comes in as a way of defusing low-level tension.

You will need:
Two or more players (an even number)
Somewhere soft to play, like a patch of grass or a large gym mat
A sock for each player

Each competitor wears one sock and the challenge is to take the opposing person's sock. In a large group you can have more than one battle going at once, or make a circle around those battling to create an atmosphere much like that of the sporting arena or boxing match. It's all in fun, so it doesn't get too heavy.

Obviously, if your kids are ready to give each other a proper beating, this game might not be the best idea, but it's useful for distracting them and defusing low-level tension. If the grown-ups are joining in, maybe pitch two kids against one adult! (I know that doesn't seem fair but you are bigger.) If you have enough time, I would always go for the best-of-three – swapping the sock from one foot to the other in each round.

LEARN THE LANGUAGE OF PLAY

At one level or another, children will always tell us what they are really feeling – even if this isn't always obvious at first, or comes across as disruptive behaviour. To have a successful, productive and healthy relationship with them, we must respect their wishes and look for the clues behind the ways in which they communicate.

I always recommend creating boundaries in play so that it is clear to everyone where they stand and then enforcing those boundaries through an energy exchange that leaves children feeling uplifted and encouraged. Play is not about time management; play is the language of childhood – and if we wish to support children on their path to adulthood, enabling them to explore every facet of their personalities, we must learn to speak that language fluently.

WALK THE POSITIVITY TRAIL

Storytelling is one of the oldest traditions in the history of humanity, and one of the most powerful. This version is a "living story", which means that the participants get to experience the story physically, rather than passively, and to re-enact key scenes. If the story is one of increasing positivity, or has messages that uplift or inspire, it can be an incredibly effective tool for rewriting some of the narratives that these children have been told, or told themselves, about their own lives.

You will need:
A big bag of mixed buttons (to use as hidden treasure)
A container for the buttons
Additional props (optional)
Plenty of space in which to play

Step 1. Pick a concept and a theme: when creating a living story, plan it in advance and pick an underlying concept, such as facing fear, loneliness, not feeling good enough or standing up to bullies, which you know presents a challenge to the children who will be taking part. Weave your story around this core concept as part of a themed quest to discover hidden treasure. Your theme could be pirates or explorers, for example.

Step 2. Plan out a very clear structure: map out a very simple structure (because the actions themselves will flesh out the narrative), with key scenes for the kids to enact. Create a magical and imaginative adventure that will take you to the heart of the issue without being patronizing, or with an obvious agenda. In a story about facing fears, for instance, these could be episodes such as "escaping the sinking sands of doom", "exploring the haunted caves" and "crossing Snap-Rope Bridge". After two or three earlier challenges, plan a key scene that embodies the story's underlying theme.

Step 3. Embellish the scenes: each scene should create a different atmosphere from the one before it, with a clear physical action (such as wading through gloopy sand or tottering over a shaky bridge). Where possible, accompany each scene with a specific vocal noise for everyone to make, such as the squelch of sand or the shrieking of bats. Make it funny as well as a bit scary or challenging.

Step 4. Include team work: weave in activities that encourage teamwork, such as making a human chain to cross the sands, or choosing a leader to guide them through the caves. These not so subtle but very clear messages about teamwork and helping people are a brilliant way to introduce the notion of community.

Step 5. Have treasure for them to find: after you have been through three or four hazards, it will be time to discover the treasure. Your stash of buttons should be hidden inside a container of some sort, such as a teapot or box, for them to discover at the appropriate point in the story.

Step 6. Start to live the story: it's time to play by leading everyone through each scene of the story, encouraging them to engage their imaginations by following your example. (Props are optional.) Let them see you act through a whole range of emotions – from bravery to fear. As some of these scenes might be scary, keep reassuring the children that you are there with them and it's funny in some way. Be aware of when the children are ready to move on.

Step 7. Get to the heart of the matter: Once you have been through a couple of challenges together and you know everyone is completely engaged, give them the option to turn back; by this point they should be keen to continue. They will also have loosened up and, having found a way to get through the earlier challenges, they will have experienced reassurance – which will allow you to enter into the more difficult part, creating the opportunity for them to speak about something that might be affecting their lives in the real world, once more following your lead.

Step 8. Discover the treasure: once they have faced their challenges through the story, it's time to bridge the gap between the worlds of the imagination and reality, and transfer the magic across by discovering the treasure. Explain that, while the treasure might just look like buttons, in fact they have magical properties. This should fit the themes of your story (for example, in a pirate-themed story about fear, you could explain that each of the buttons has been taken from a famous sea-rover and gives the gift of bravery).

Step 9. Activate the buttons: having shared out the buttons, ask everyone to raise them in a fist above their head. Next, ask them to squeeze the button, close their eyes and picture the thing that upsets them most. Tell them to take a deep breath and imagine it getting much bigger. Now, as they breathe out, let those upsetting feelings go as the picture gets much smaller, while the power from the button flows down their arms and beams into them, filling them up.

Step 10. End big: encourage them to celebrate the end of the adventure by making lots of noise, maybe dancing or shouting, to ground all that excitement and energy.

Step 11. Use the buttons: tell each child they can harness the button's power by carrying it with them or sewing it into an item of clothing. If they're scared of the dark, perhaps they can sew the button into their dressing gown. Or if they're anxious about failing at sport, perhaps they can sew it secretly inside of their sports kit. If they're scared of the school bully, they can sew the button inside of their blazer. It's also a badge of honour: they belong now to a crew of adventurers.

The Flying Seagull Project team have played this story with more groups of kids than I can remember and I cannot tell you how many emails we receive from parents, telling us that their little girl or boy no longer feels so afraid because they have their button and know they're part of our crew.

MAKE MAGIC HAPPEN BY EXPOSING ILLUSIONS

Adults who engage the hearts and souls of children who look up to them are in the most unbelievably powerful position. It is our role to make sure we let children know that any damage that's already been done – any fears or insecurities they carry, any external pressures that make them feel small or not valuable – aren't real. While they might feel real and overwhelming, we have to help them to understand that everything can be climbed over and overcome and that just by being themselves they are already totally and utterly brilliant.

I will repeat, and I would ask you to repeat this to yourself too, when it comes to children: "There is no such thing as not good enough. There is no such thing as not good enough." Repeat ten times with me – come on now! – "There is no such thing as not good enough." This message is essential when working with children and something to remember in everything we do.

LEARNING TO FIND THE SILVER LINING

It's a strange fact of life that it's often easier to focus on the negatives in life than otherwise. It just seems easier for us to be judgemental and impatient. Being English, I'm sometimes told it's a Western, cultural thing, and having worked in some pretty depressing places yet finding some of the most positive people on earth there, this could well be true – at least partly.

In West Africa's biggest slum, Ghana's infamous Agbogbloshie community, I found the response to play and the slightest encouragement so overwhelmingly positive that it caught me off guard. Night and day, the air there was filled with thick, black, toxic smoke from the burning of cables to get at the copper inside. Between the shacks and lean-tos ran raw sewage and garbage. The community struggled in nearly every way possible, with challenges from malnutrition to pestilence and of course overwhelming poverty. Yet here we were hard pressed to find a single unhappy face. The moment we arrived in the morning, a procession of dancing, singing, happy children (and a few parents too) would join us and parade with us from show to show with sparkling eyes and that characteristic Ghanaian charm.

In some ways, it's pointless to draw comparisons, yet I think there is definitely something we can learn from the Ghanaian resilience to adversity, and their determination to be happy in spite of their challenges. Life will never stop throwing us good and bad news every day, but how we respond to this allows us to be in charge of how much we suffer. Looked at the other way, there's no such thing as good luck, just a hearty amount of optimism regardless of the situation.

Today, in the West, the rates of conditions such as anxiety, depression and other well-being related afflictions are higher than ever before, and sadly so too are the numbers of suicides among certain sectors of society, such as teenagers. I feel deeply that the temptation of pessimism is something we should move away from as a society; and, as always, these habits are formed in childhood. Somehow we are failing to learn in our youth how to make it through hard times.

While I'm not suggesting that play will solve everything, it's a good starting point toward creating new habits, for rather than being set in stone, at least habits can be changed.

DELIGHT DETECTIVES

Delight Detectives is less of a game and more of a community-building activity, whether that community consists of family, classmates or colleagues at work (it's a good activity for adults too). It's a way of manoeuvring through the temptation to focus on faults and problems, and instead invites us to seek out reasons for celebration.

You will need:
Pens
Scrap paper and pins, or sticky labels
Cork board (large)
Metal bucket
Matches

Step 1. Create your Board of Brilliance and Bucket of Goodbye: put up the cork board in a prominent place and decorate it together if you like. Stick the metal bucket or bin in a corner.

Step 2. Become Delight Detectives: everyone is told to search out the good from the bad. Track down those shiny, sunny, lovely, warm, sparkly good vibes that are being held hostage by the low-ebb bandits.

Step 3. Write up the good news: when you get together at the end of a day or week, write down a brilliant thing that happened. This could be something that someone did, a fun game, the weather – whatever you thought was great. Once everyone has written something down, take turns to read out your notes and stick them on the Board of Brilliance.

Step 4. Bin the bad stuff: those things that you didn't enjoy, that upset you or were just rubbish are to go in the Bucket of Goodbye. Write them down on scraps of paper, but don't read them out. Just screw them up and throw them into the bucket while saying goodbye out loud and in your thoughts.

Step 5. Burn away negativity: when everyone's bad stuff is in the bin, the group leader finds a safe place (preferably outside) to burn the notes. As the smoke vanishes, the negatives will also go up in smoke. Everyone makes the agreement that once it's gone, it's gone.

This activity is only symbolic of course, and not proven to remove all stress, but it fosters a long-term celebration of the good stuff.

No Such Thing as Too Much Encouragement

While fake praise is patronizing and kids have a second sense when it comes to being spoken down to, there is no such thing as too much genuine encouragement. A child knows if they are brilliant at something or not, so our job as adults is to take away the value judgements system around being good enough or not good enough at that thing. There are plenty of positive, compassionate and encouraging things that we can say which are truthful.

The desire to be comforting by offering exaggerated praise instead creates a sense of dishonesty which, in the end, doesn't provide the comfort it was intended to. By now you might have guessed that I prefer an authentic and equality-based communication between adults and children. As I've touched on before, this doesn't mean speaking to them like I would one of my adult friends, but it does mean showing the same level of respect for them when explaining things, comforting them or encouraging their work.

POOP SANDWICH

Thankfully the Poop Sandwich is nowhere near as disgusting as it sounds, so don't worry! It's a structure for giving constructive feedback. People are afraid of criticism, especially children, and if you're not careful their very first response is defensiveness, which switches off any potential dialogue. When we use the Poop Sandwich, we put the negative (i.e. the poop) between two positive slices of bread.

For example, if I wanted to tell you that I think you could improve on listening to other members of the group, I would open that feedback with something positive. I might say your energy and your commitment are fantastic and I'm really grateful for how much excitement you bring to activities. Then I'd explain that sometimes I think it might be good if you tried to make sure you listen to everybody else's ideas right to the end before adding any more of that great energy into the mix. I would finish on another positive, and make this personal, such as that you're very funny, so when you've heard everybody else out, please make sure to tell us a joke or two.

The ingredients of the sandwich are thus as follows:

1. The compliment, linked to the activity or behaviour that the criticism has arisen from.
2. The constructive feedback, aka poop.
3. The second compliment, which should be personal, such as their sense of humour, their kindness or generosity. Making this something about them personally helps to heal any detrimental effect the criticism has had on their confidence. This is not undermining the feedback you've given them, but to re-establish that it does not devalue them; in fact, as we've seen, our weaknesses are part of our strength.

KEEP YOUR COOL

Any parent or person who works with children knows that, no matter what, there are going to be moments where our patience is tested. Children have the unique ability to find the one thing that really drives you mad, and then to do that thing, over and over and over again. They also have the unique ability to find the exact moment to annoy you the most by unleashing their awesome talent for provocation. However, we still have a duty to control our response. Simply saying we won't lose our patience, is not enough. We need to develop a strategy to ensure that whenever our patience is tested we are able to return to a state of generosity, warmth and, where appropriate, professionalism.

In my work, my team and I have had the honour of working with some incredibly lively and boundary-testing children. I think this is a fantastic thing, although challenging, because somehow – in spite of all of the effort and pressure for them to behave – they still won't conform. This means that, while their energy might be a bit misdirected at times, they still have the confidence to remain independent and continue to question everything.

So how do we make sure that in play and at home, in school, in the car, in the supermarket, on the train, at a wedding and all the other places where children will decide to test out their independence, we are able to maintain a degree of patience? And how do we teach our children to be patient too? Patient with each other, patient with us, patient with the people that they will meet throughout their lives – from work colleagues to so-called authority figures? Well, at The Flying Seagull Project, I have developed something called "patience training".

PATIENCE TRAINING

The purpose of patience training is to create a simulated and somewhat exaggerated environment to test everyone's patience – and what's more, it's fun!

You will need:

A newspaper

Items of mass distraction: e.g. inflatable hammer, small water pistol, bike horn, basically anything is perfect that you could use to antagonize someone without causing any pain

A sound system or portable speaker (must be loud)

Very loud, annoying or aggravating music (I recommend thrash metal)

Step 1. Start the audition: this is the participant's big chance to become a newsreader. To do so, he or she has to cross the room while reading out loud, in a clear and calm voice, a newspaper article from top to bottom.

Step 2. Disrupt the audition: everyone else has to stop the participant from completing the story. They are not allowed to touch the newspaper; however they are allowed to touch the would-be newsreader as long as it is not in an aggressive way. Tapping, poking or prodding with an inflatable hammer are perfectly acceptable.

Step 3. Turn up the music: the noise and energy in the room should be very high and very caricatured. If you are facilitating this activity, you must make sure that there is a comedic edge to what is happening, and that nobody is becoming too upset and stressed out.

Step 4. Offer revenge: once the first audition has taken place, you announce it is time for Round Two or, as you like to call it, "revenge". Repeat the activity until everybody had a turn.

Step 5. Talk it over: at the end, have a discussion which gives everyone a chance to voice precisely what annoyed them the most, and ask them to write down any ways that they found to get through the experience that they can share with the others.

GAMES TO MEET CHALLENGE WITH A SMILE

These games help change the frowns into smiles, and release a positive charge of happiness into potentially stormy situations.

GAME 1: MY FRIEND [BOB] IS A TOTAL LEGEND BECAUSE...

As we've seen, words have impact, yet we mainly focus on the negative ones. To be emotionally developed, we need to build a vocabulary of praise and to get in the habit of using it. With that in mind, The Flying Seagull Project has created the game "My friend Bob is a total legend because…" It's a great game to play to help us recognize the good in each other, which I believe allows us to recognize more fully the good in ourselves. This also makes it especially suited to groups where there might be a tendency toward hostile or negative behaviour.

You will need:
Two or more participants
Many, many words!

Step 1. Choose somebody to praise: instead of "Bob", use the name of whoever you've chosen. If you're part of a group, perhaps choose a different person to praise each week, or pass the praise to the left, right or across the circle.

Step 2. Let the praising begin: start short, such as simply: "My friend [Bob] is a total legend because he's kind." Nobody is allowed to say anything negative or rude, even if it's funny and meant in a friendly way.

Step 3. Make the praise increasingly elaborate: the next person in the group has to make their praise longer and more ornate than the person before. (Use your fingers to count the words if you're not sure.) So, for example, you might say, "My friend [Amy] is a total legend because she is one of the cleverest, loveliest and funniest people I've ever met – and that includes all the people I've read about in books." However, you can't repeat anything that anyone else has said. As you go round the group, make the praise increasingly over-the-top and funny.

The more ludicrous and long-winded the answers are, the more fun this game is. However, it also asks you to dig deep into your vocabulary and, even though it's jocular, you really have to start to examine the person carefully from the position of finding positive and complimentary things to say about them.

GAME 2: HIGH-SPEED COMPLIMENT COMPETITION

This is another game that invites us to focus on the positive. It's a great, quick-fire way to introduce some fizzing energy into a group in the middle of other activities. It is played very similarly to a word association game but the challenge is to come up with as many nice things to say as possible.

Step 1. Split people into pairs or groups of three: the people in the same team sit or stand facing each other.

Step 2. Take turns complimenting each other: each person says a compliment, followed quickly by their team member replying with theirs. The comments can be as ridiculous as you like, as long as they're not rude: "you're as beautiful as a bowl of custard" is acceptable, "your butt smells like roses" not so much. Other than this, there are no wrong answers in this one. However, like a word association game, you can't say "errrrm", and there should be no pauses or repetition of compliments.

GAME 3: PASS THE SQUAWK

This is essentially a memory game, pass the parcel and a dance-off mixed into one. It's a great game for improving the mood of the players and for helping them to overcome any insecurities or reservations.

You will need:
Five or more participants
Enough room to stand in a circle and move about a bit
Quick thinking, imagination and a good memory

Step 1. Each person has to identify themselves with a "squawk" that is unique to them: each squawk comprises of three elements – body, sound and face.

Example 1
Movement: flap arms and stick out your bum.
Sound: shriek like a seagull.
Face: pout your mouth to look like a beak.
Example 2
Movement: stand on one leg.
Sound: blow a raspberry.
Face: grin from ear to ear.

The reason there are three elements is that this multiple focus has the effect of reducing the self-awareness of those playing, as they're concentrating too much on creating each bit. The challenge of remembering your squawk as well as other people's is enough to take you out of your reservations.

Step 2. Get everyone to share their squawks: going round the circle, ask each person to demonstrate their moves. Then ask everyone else to copy that squawk a few times. Test them by pointing randomly at somebody and asking the rest of the group to do their squawk. Once you are confident that everybody knows each other's moves, but not so well that they don't have to think about it, it's time to play.

Step 3. Start playing Pass the Squawk: begin by doing the squawk of one of your team-mates. This makes them the active player. As quick as they can, they have to make the identifying squawk of another person in the group to "pass it on". In the first round you can allow for a bit of pausing and befuddlement.

Step 4. Introduce new rules: explain that any hesitation, or doing your own move, or getting one of the faces or moves wrong, means that the player is out and has to sit down and wait for the next round. (The great thing about this game is even if you are out, you have a hilarious opportunity to watch the rest of your group, family or friends struggle to remember to bark like a dog whilst winking and doing ballet.) The game ends when it's either too funny to keep playing, or there are only two people left.

The speed of this game should increase incrementally each round that you play it, and I would recommend playing three rounds in one sitting. Also, if everyone has to choose a new squawk each game, toward the third round you will find that the squawks have an increasing amount of nonsense involved, as all the obvious choices will have gone. So the first round is simply about remembering, the second round is faster with no hesitations, whereas the third round is superfast without getting any of the three elements of the squawk wrong. As an added extra, if the children don't think the adult has formed a suitable squawk, they are allowed to demand a re-squawk!

THE CHALLENGE OF REAL PLAY

As parents and play leaders, one of our many roles is to encourage, embolden and empower children; to give them the grounding that enables them to gain an understanding both of themselves and of society as a whole; and to find where their path in life will take them. We have to metaphorically hold these children's souls, their thoughts and their hearts – and to do this all whilst running a game.

Play shapes how children understand the world, how they research their surroundings, how they form and break bonds of friendship, and how they explore their strengths and weaknesses. If you are bold and courageous enough to place yourself in the role of play leader or parent, you must be prepared for the responsibility that comes with this. The responsibility we have to children is to be 100 per cent present for them and 100 per cent observant and respectful of *who* they are. Through Real Play, we can help them grow as people and revolutionize the future.

CHAPTER 8

START YOUR OWN REAL PLAY REVOLUTION

"The best thing you can offer is yourself and, if you're authentic, it's always enough."

The choice of game, quality of equipment, location, weather – pretty much all external factors – mean nothing in the end. As we've seen, what kids really want is *you*. They want you to see them fully and to show yourself in full range. If you try to hide from them, they will know, or at the very least sense something is up. While they might not yet be in the habit of explaining, justifying or intellectualizing a situation or behaviour, they can still perceive what's in front of them. If you want children to follow your lead and to start your own Real Play Revolution, play to all your strengths to earn their respect. Learn from your heroes – then become one.

Many of us are lucky enough to have a childhood hero or two whose influence has stayed with us over the years. Mine were Mrs King and Dr Hewitt. Mrs King was my art teacher in middle school, and the unofficial head of encouragement for us all;

whereas Dr Hewitt was my physics teacher in upper school. Mrs King was playful and, unusually for teachers at the time, we knew that she was always being herself, not putting on a part in the classroom. Dr Hewitt approached his lessons with a passion that meant that all of us felt excited by the subject.

Like many people, I had a mixed relationship with school. I was born with an ear defect, which meant I had just under 20 per cent of my hearing, yet I started formal school a year early, so I really only understood it in terms of play to begin with. At first, with the support of speech therapists who also used play in their work with me, I flourished. Then trouble struck. There came a point where an over-confident chatterbox, with a hunger for debate and an instinct for humour, was no longer considered a positive addition to the class, but a disruption and nuisance. This led to my getting removed from classrooms and being told to quieten down and follow the rules. I quickly earned a pretty bad reputation with some of the staff and fell into the group labelled "naughty kids".

Then along came Mrs King, whose methods were completely different. Although her lessons were planned, they were never the same twice, and each one moved at a pace that meant we never stagnated. She made me feel that she recognized me, at the age of nine, as a person, with humour, respect and playfulness. Later, when I was 11 years old, Dr Hewitt showed me that while physics might be a traditional subject, it doesn't have to be taught in a traditional way. Rather than impose an academic and formalized method on us, he tried to engage the class by creating an environment where we felt energized and accepted without judgement. That isn't to say he didn't tease us. He accepted my high energy and created an imaginary disease around it, which he called Perrinitis (my surname being Perrin).

For both of these teachers, their classes didn't aim to create a room full of physicians or art scholars, but to share the depth of one of life's wonders that had gripped them so fully. They were willing to be completely present and reveal themselves in their classes. Neither of them were without personal flaws or weaknesses, yet rather than trying to pretend to be anything than what they were, they were REAL – and we all loved them for that.

To lead your own Real Play Revolution, you have to believe that you too can become someone's hero, role model, mentor – or simply act as a place of safety in stormy waters. In moments of potential challenge and crisis, if you are authentic in what you do, you will find it much easier to redirect high energy into positive outcomes.

CLOWN CRISIS RESOLUTION SYSTEMS

As part of our mentorship in play with children, we have to be there for them in bad times as well as good. Whether it's at home with the family, in a classroom or any other place where people assemble, there are inevitably and unavoidably going to be times of tension. In the home, tension can occur between siblings or parents or just about everyone. Some days you wake up and you're all spoiling for it! You can feel there's a row on the horizon. In the classroom, this tension can grow over time between members of the class or sometimes teachers, and everybody's stress levels rise above what is healthy for us.

The point, I suppose, is that life is generally a bit stressful – and when we come together with lots of different people, we're adding together a lot of individual stresses, which creates the possibility for an outburst. As we saw in Chapter 7, when children express themselves in this way, and become angry, rebellious or aggressive, we have to understand that it is the communication of a whole wellspring of intense emotions. Anger is normally the by-product of frustration and frustration is normally the by-product of confusion, for example; whereas aggression can often result from a child feeling attacked or embarrassed.

While I make no claims to be a child psychologist, I firmly believe that expecting adult behaviour and adult rationale, or insisting on these from children, is not only going to be ineffective but is also going to cause distance and generate more tension in the relationships between the people involved. As mentors, we have been able to meet these moments of tension in a slightly different way – and I would like to share some ideas of how you can create a humorous and comedic infrastructure that allows people to feel the emotions they have, while keeping everyone else smiling while they work them through.

At first this might look like a very flippant approach, but I genuinely believe it can transform tricky households or tough groups. For it to work, you'll have to commit properly to taking part and honouring the agreement that you make.

COMEDIC COMMITMENT CONTRACTS

These are binding documents between you and others, in which you agree to commit to a comedic approach to crisis resolution. These contracts mean that you have publicly promised to play along, in front of those you love or respect, to perform a certain action (such as wear a silly hat, eat beans for a whole weekend as a new tradition, make a fart noise in a museum etc.) when particular circumstances arise – and, come hell or high water, you will not say no when the moment comes. You wouldn't break a promise to somebody you love, and by drawing up a Comedic Commitment Contract, you're granting play the same level of importance.

Plus, it's funny.

Step 1. Draw up your contract: sit down and negotiate the terms with all parties concerned. The contract should cover the following aspects:

- Title of contract.
- Date valid from/to.
- Names of those concerned.
- Terms of delivery: how the action will be delivered; for example, "When the red button is pressed, I'll squawk like a chicken in full voice – regardless of location."
- Why this been agreed: a simple but meaningful reason, for example, "Because as a family we want to play more together." This is pretty important, as it's the motivation behind making the contract.
- Punitive measure for breaking the contract: this could be a forfeit but considering one of you has just refused to participate, you'll probably refuse to honour this measure too. Instead, I recommend a clause that involves emotional blackmail, such as: "Failure to honour the contract will result in very sad children who don't think their daddy loves them enough to play properly." Heavy, I know, but this is a contract after all...
- Exceptions to the rule: for example, "not when we're at granny's house", "not at the vet's or during exams", etc.
- Signatures (including that of an independent witness).

You will find an example of a Comedic Commitment Contract at the back of this book, as well as a blank template that you can cut out and use as the basis of any of the contracts described below or one that you have made up yourself.

Step 2. Enforce the contract: once the contract has been discussed and negotiated, drawn up and signed by everybody, it becomes binding. It's the mark of everyone's commitment to honour and respect play, love, friendship and affection above anything else that might be stressing you out. So it ought to be treated with all the sincerity and poignancy of a promise. It is an agreement of nonsense – and these should never be broken or ignored.

DO NOT PRESS BUTTON

First of all you need to build a press-able red button with DO NOT PRESS written on it. This can be as simple as drawing on the cardboard from inside a cereal box, or as elaborate as a chicken-wire, papier-mâché invention – but it has to be big, red and able to be pushed.

At the beginning of the week, you and the children sign a Comedic Commitment Contract. The contract states that at any point over a specified period of time (I would recommend a week), the participants named within the contract have to perform a certain task whenever the red button is pressed. For example, I might write in my contract that if I press the button, everybody had to do 30 seconds of clucking and waving their arms about like a chicken flapping its wings.

I recommend adding a couple of clauses to the contract, such as including some limits in terms of public decency and no foul language. For example, the word "poo" is extremely popular amongst five-year-olds and might not be something you wish to be contractually obligated to shout out while doing jumping splits in the cereal aisle of your local supermarket once that button is pressed!

Likewise, you can add restrictions as to whether the button may be used no more than twice a day, for example, or only two times in public a week. It doesn't really matter – the point is a conspiratorial bond of silliness: a commitment to be playful and to put yourself on the line – and to do it in a big way. To show that you are willing to honour an agreement, no matter how silly and foolish it may be, just for the fun of it; because it doesn't matter what anybody else thinks, it doesn't matter what judgements they make. This is especially important especially if your kids or students have reasons (which all young people believe they do) to think that society may be judging them in a way that is negative.

BEAT THE GRUMP TURKEY HAT REDUCTION SYSTEM

The truth is, sometimes we all have a reason to feel grumpy. We didn't get enough sleep, we had a hard time at work, somebody ate our chocolate bar, we didn't enjoy dinner ... Yet, with the best will in the world, no grump has ever been transformed by having their grumpiness highlighted by other people. It is a scientific fact that nobody has ever been made to feel better by being told that they're grumpy. Instead, it's almost 99.9 per cent certain that they will become increasingly grumpy as a result of being told how grumpy they are.

At this point there is a way out – and it's called The Grump Turkey Hat. As with all Clown Crisis Resolution Systems, this must be agreed in advance, in a time of calm. The agreement is called the Turkey Hat Grump Destroyer.

For this, you will need a stuffed turkey hat (there are some inexpensive options available online) and to make a contractual commitment that whoever is being grumpy will wear it until their mood improves. Hopefully this won't take long, as it's difficult to remain a grump with a turkey on your head – and at least it's amusing for those around the grump to see such a moody face being sat on by a turkey.

RED NOSE ROW REDUCTION AND RESOLUTION SYSTEM

When you find that a row is about to erupt, it's time to act. It's time for The Red Nose Row Reduction and Resolution System. This contract can be used in the classroom group setting; however, it's better aimed at adults, as some children who are reacting emotionally might find it humiliating to be painted in front of their peers. It can also be used as a preventative measure, when a disagreement is building. If you get the parties involved to sit opposite each other, with their noses painted red, and encourage an over-the-top yelling match between them, this will without fail result in fits of laughter.

To use it, draw up and sign the contract for this system prior to the start of any arguments. Then keep some red face paint and sponges to hand. The next time that people start to row, one of you can says, "Red Nose Resolution System activate!" You then paint each other's noses red and carry on arguing if so desired.

That said, it's very difficult to yell when your nose is red – and the act of painting each other's noses is sensory and normally will re-connect you to whoever you are arguing with, which means the argument will move toward a close. If the argument doesn't finish, at least everyone looks ridiculous – and if the children are unfortunate enough to be caught up in a row between their parents, for example, they will be treated to a quite amusing image of two angry adults with red noses.

The only rule is you are not allowed to say no if the other person calls for a Red Nose Resolution. The point is, in the moment that your nose is painted red, you are angry, you don't want to play, and you've forgotten precisely where you are, who you are and why you are. Your argument might be about something quite serious; however, when used in a timely manner, the Red Nose Resolution System has been proven to defuse stern and hostile output.

If the situation is very serious, of course you must be responsible about calling for a Red Nose Resolution, as it might just turn the receiver of the red nose into a red nose monster of madness, so be cautious and be respectful. This contract is meant to foster a playful, warm connection and be a way of alleviating tension – not humiliating someone. It should never be used as an act of dominance or oppression, but just a way of acknowledging the foolishness of discussing anything at screaming pitch!

WHAT'RE THE ODDS?

This game doesn't use a Comedic Commitment Contract, but it shares the same ingredient of daring as the contracts. It's also a great way to make everyone put themselves on the line.

Step 1. Set the challenge: one person asks another what are the odds that they would do something very silly and publicly embarrassing, such as: "What are the odds you'll dance like a ballerina in the middle of the dining hall at lunch break today?"
Step 2. Respond to the challenge by stating the odds: the person who has been challenged says a number, such as 50. A number like 50 is quite high and means they would find the challenge embarrassing, whereas a low number like ten means it wouldn't be that embarrassing.
Step 3. Negotiate the outcome: now, the person who set the challenge tries to persuade the other one to bring that number down, going back and forth until a new number is agreed; in this case, let's say 30. Together they count, "One, two, three ..." and then they both pick a number between 1 and 30. If they say the same number, the responder has to go and do that ballet dance in the middle of the dining hall during lunch break. If the numbers don't match the dare is simply forgotten and cannot be repeated.

My proposition, as preposterous as it is, is that adults should put themselves on the line and agree to play this game with kids. Perhaps you're on a family holiday, walking round a castle somewhere in Wales, and your little girl says, "Mummy, what are the odds that you shout the word 'bogey' as loud as you can right now?" If you play the game properly, your nerves will be real, and they will see a more human side of you than they might be used to seeing in grown-ups. And if you lose, it'll be an experience that they will genuinely remember for a long, long time to come. This activity, though flippant and silly, is a great way of equalizing the status between you and the children that you're playing with. Go on, I dare you – play a game of What're the Odds?!

FAKE NEWS! WHY NOT TELL THE TRUTH?

I think most of us probably do this already, but just in case, it's worth saying: if a child asks you a question, tell them the truth. As fun as it is to bamboozle and entertain our children with fantasy and fiction, there is a time and a place for this. When they ask you a question because they want to understand something, even if it feels that it may be difficult for them to comprehend, tell them the truth.

A rudimentary, child-shaped, non-technical truth is fine, but it should be the truth nonetheless. When it comes to our own children, most of us find it a lot easier to be honest, whereas if we are engaging with them in a professional capacity we will sometimes need to use reasonable judgement as to what it's appropriate to tell them. If this applies to you, you might want to suggest they should ask their parents or care provider instead. But, in general, the dawn of the internet means that kids can access the information they are after, so if you stall you are simply putting off a discovery that they will inevitably make, and missing an opportunity to have a reasonable, rational and safe discussion about it.

By now many of us will be familiar with the evolution of the echo chamber in social media online, whereby beliefs (however misguided) become reinforced by repetition inside a closed system. This applies too to the insane amounts of totally agenda-driven and sometimes outright untruths that belong to the world of social media. If you leave it to social media to answer a child's questions, you might regret it. A conversation and genuine discussion might still result in them having some quirky convictions, but at least they'll have thought them through first. This might be about really tricky subject such as drugs or alcohol, or it could involve complicated social issues like homelessness or global conflict or the environment.

When children ask you a question, this is an opportunity for you to explain and help them to understand the world around them. In their own way, these questions can be playful, but they are all part of the exploration and attempt to understand and therefore successfully interact with the world in which they live. So no more fake news!

HAVE YOU EVER PLAYED "ACTUAL REALITY"?

In a world where all of life seems to be found on the internet, it's worth introducing kids to this amazing new game. It's incredible – you've never seen graphics like it! It's called Actual Reality! It's so real, you can literally touch the things you're playing with, and the other players are so life-like that they are actually there – and you can really talk to them!

Now, I want to make something clear that I'm not against computer games, or against kids playing on tablets and having a bit of screen time. I'm certainly not against some amazing new games that try to crossover between computer games and actual play. There is an absolutely perfect place for computer games, and that is during restful entertainment, like on a wet and windy day when your mates come round and sit in the lounge together; but this is not play, it is gaming, and as such we have to monitor it as much as we would monitor social media computer time.

We also have to acknowledge that there is an addictive edge in the way that our children interact with certain computer games. Let's be honest – the digital world and the world of social media and gaming have become dangerously intrusive in our lives and affect our very social fabric, even when we're supposed to be spending time together. I recently had a meal with seven friends, and at one point everybody was staring at their phone. For our children to understand and to manage this digital habit of ours, we cannot make the mistake of thinking that playing a football game on a screen is the same as playing a game in the garden with friends.

With computers, even with so-called sports games, you do not even get the health benefits of real play. Instead of waving a bit of plastic around on the spot, why not play a real game of tennis instead? And that's my point with the kids: yes, they can play "active games", such as exploring a digital garden to find the things that grow there, but that's not as good as going into a real garden and breathing in fresh air, filling your brain with oxygen and exploring the natural world with your fingertips, smelling the flowers rather than reading about what they smell like. Today, one of the most revolutionary play suggestions is simply to go outside with friends and play a good, old traditional game like Bulldog – and enjoy the liberation of mind, body and creativity this brings. You won't get that experience with a computer game; you simply grow numb.

Moving into adolescence, this reliance on, and addiction to, screens presents even more dangers. Today, more young people than ever appear to be suffering from depression-related mental illness and suicide rates are higher than ever – yet this is a time when social media is meant to be bringing us all together. The strange and peculiarly disconnected world online, where we can create avatar-style representations of ourselves for the scrutiny of others and where success is based on how many "likes" or shares we receive, is toxic and dangerous. There can be a very real sense of anxiety as we wait for the digital approval of those within our social media networks, which is known as "text-pectation". The normalization of the world of social media and its offerings is already being shown to have negative consequences in terms of our self-confidence and social interconnectivity. Quite simply, it doesn't make us feel good when most of our friends only exist online, and we don't even know what they really look like because all of their pictures have been altered.

I'll say it once and I'll say it loud (even if it loses me a few friends): no-one cares what you had for dinner, and we certainly don't need to see a picture of it. Put down your phone and be yourself – without waiting for a hundred people to "like" you online.

My argument is simply that virtual reality in any format is nowhere near as good as Actual Reality. It's time to get your knees muddy again.

The encouraging thing is that there seems to be a new movement toward limiting screen time and encouraging outdoor play. So for our shared revolution, let's take a next step into Actual Reality – and celebrate this wonderful world and all its fun.

REWRITE THE YEAR!

Traditions and celebrations are a truly essential part of our social fabric. Growing up, I remember clearly the excitement I would feel when summer arrived, because it meant that carnival day would soon be here. I have vivid memories of bonfire night in our town too, and occasions like the harvest festival. All these celebrations all form part of a repetitive and therefore familiar structure within the year and in our lives. Growing up, these events are more than just dates in the diary; they become experiences that we can recall each year – and look forward to in the year ahead.

There are many reasons for it, but it seems that many traditions are disappearing in our modern age, so my solution is to create our own new traditions and celebrate brand new ceremonies.

You will need:
Wall calendar or chart
Pack of multi-coloured pens
Heartfelt commitment to family foolery

Step 1. Choose a day to celebrate: this can be any date you like. Make sure everybody in the family or group is included and gets to choose a date too. There's no reason why you can't choose a day for each month, or even more if you're that sort of family.

Step 2. Decide on the name and the celebration: each person decides what their day is going to be called and a unique way to celebrate it. This could be as silly as "Thomas the Tank Engine Day", when you all have to dress like the Fat Controller; or Baked Bean Sunday, when you have to eat baked meals with every meal. Or it could be significant, like Grandparents Day, to remember grandparents who aren't with you anymore by visiting places that you used to enjoy together. Or it could be Slippers Day, High-Five Wednesday or Justin Bieber Week!

Step 3. Write it on the calendar in bright colours: you could make a calendar on a whiteboard (although the temptation to rub out and scribble a note to your partner to not forget milk might be too high). Or use an old-fashioned wall calendar. Fill it with all the weird and wonderful significant dates that you've decided upon. Once you have listed each occasion in the calendar, write out the details so that everyone understands what the celebration includes.

Step 4. Celebrate: perhaps create special costumes, cook specific food, and even make up songs for the occasion that everybody has to learn. It's up to you what you do, but at the very least there should be one thing that you all do together on that day of celebration, be it taking a dip in the sea in January or synchronized eating of a spoonful of peanut butter. Make it personal, make it important – and hold on to the silly days of your traditions every year for as long as you can.

Of course, if there are still traditional annual celebrations where you live, take your kids along to them. Whether they are faith-based, or historically significant, or simply something that your town has always done – doesn't really matter. You don't have to be aligned with the motivation behind a particular event to become a part of the community that celebrates it.

When The Flying Seagull Project was working on the Syrian border in Lebanon, we were present during Ramadan and Eid. It was fun, and though none of the team identifies as Muslim, we had the warmest and most welcoming experience, enjoying the food, music and energy in the community. I don't think that taking part in a celebration that is linked to a different faith or another aspect that you don't share compromises either side; it only builds a bond between us all that includes these differences. The main thing is taking a moment to recognize something that we love and celebrate it with those that we love.

THE KEY INGREDIENTS FOR YOUR REAL PLAY REVOLUTION

Whatever games you play, and if there's nothing else that you take away from this book, there are three key ingredients that I'd like you to remember:

ENERGY

We've looked at the importance of energy time and again in this book, but I still can't stress it enough: it doesn't matter what exercises you do, what games you know, or how well-planned your sessions or playtimes are – none of it means anything without the right energy. An energy that is clear, present and committed. An energy that is playful, excited and enthusiastic. An energy that is bombastic, slightly bonkers and full of beans.

To help you connect with this energy, you might have to find something that triggers its release in you. This could be anything that stimulates the wilder side of your personality. It could be joyful video footage from *Mary Poppins*; it could be a photograph, like Albert Einstein sticking his tongue out. Or it might be a musical soundtrack, or even a whole playlist uniquely chosen by your inner rabble-rouser.

Whatever it is, use it to get you in the energetic zone. Think of it as being a bit like a lumberjack sharpening his axe, or a surgeon preparing her tools, or an artist making sure the paints are ready for creating a masterpiece. As a play person, you have to make sure that your tools are sharp, your energy is high and your smile is ready. This applies to being a parent, or a teacher, or anyone else who is in a position of influence emotionally over children. Check yourself before you walk into your classroom or arrive home from work. Check that you're ready to be the playful one, and make their day magical.

CLARITY

Children's minds are racing and full of fantastical thoughts at all times. There are so many things going on that in order for them to fully understand and participate in play and other activities, things have to be clear. This doesn't mean those things can't be playful, abstract or silly as well. But it means that you have to be specific and there has to be clarity in your instructions and in the structure of the games in order for them to understand fully and engage with them.

So keep it clear and make it precise. That framework or skeleton of precision gives you the opportunity to hang as much nonsense off it as you feel like. But if it's just 100 per cent nonsense, then some children will find this more irritating than entertaining.

SIMPLICITY

The purpose of play is not to invent the most complex, intricate and progressive ideas. Those things may come, and what we gain from play in the long term are the foundations that allow us to build these more delicate structures on top. For play to have its true feeling of liberation and freedom, it needs to be simple. Many of the games, if not all of the games, that I've shared in the book are in no way clever or academically enhancing, or even particularly tricky to learn. They're simple: for instance, you run around when the music plays and you stop when it stops. And for that reason they have endured the test of time.

This is because knowing how something works makes us feel good. And if something is super simple, we don't have to waste our energy trying to figure out what we're meant to do; instead we can fully immerse ourselves in the experience of actually doing it. We can be racing across the field in a game of Amoeba Tag (see page 66), for example, and our worries are no longer present. This is because we have partnered the cognitive with the physical with the personality. They all merge together in one experience and one sensation – and this is what I call "Real Play".

GAMES TO MAKE YOU GET INVOLVED!

The following three games are super-traditional; the difference here is that I'd like you to make them intergenerational. This means that I'd expect there to be as many adults playing as there are children, and for mixed partnerships rather than parents paired with parents and kids with kids. "But," I hear you say, "in some of the challenges it simply isn't really physically possible!" Good – this isn't about what's possible or probable; this is about trying, playing and putting yourself in the mix.

GAME 1: INTERGENERATIONAL, THREE-LEGGED, TWO-ARMED, DOUBLE-HEADED MONSTER RACE

This game is all about teamwork, but in this version it's also about making it personal, and really getting involved.

You will need:

Four or more participants – even numbers of adults to kids
A lawn or park to play in
Scarves to tie everyone's legs together

Step 1. Pair up into teams: ideally the pairs should be intergenerational, with an adult and child.

Step 2. Tie your legs together: using something soft, like a scarf, tie one team member's right leg to the other person's left leg at the ankle. Make sure it's knotted tight enough to stay on, but not so tight that it hurts. Each pair will have to tuck one arm behind the other for support, meaning there will be only two arms visible.

Step 3. Mark out the race track: define the length of race using jumpers or any other sort of marker, such as trees or bushes.

Step 4. On your marks …: on "go", everyone races from one end of the track to the other, making as graceful a monster as you can.

GAME 2: WILL-IT-WORK WHEELBARROW WOBBLE RACE

Wheelbarrow racing is another classic; however, it has gradually faded away over the years due to reports of grazed knees and other horrific injuries! I never liked grazing my knees as a kid, but it happened – and I survived. With this in mind, I give you this warning: you might graze your knee or even get grass stains on your elbows if you play this game. Don't say I didn't warn you!

You will need:
Four or more players (must be an even number)
A lawn or park to play in
Strong arms

Step 1. Get ready: with your partner: line up on the start line (which can be invisible or marked with jumpers). The first person is going to be the wheelbarrow and needs to lay on their front with their hands on the floor, a bit like doing a press-up. The second partner stands upright behind them, and lifts up the ankles of the first person off the ground, to turn them into a wheelbarrow.

Step 2. Go ...: to race, the person who is the wheelbarrow walks their hands forward, whilst their feet are being held up by their partner, as quickly as they can. Race all the way to one end and then, swap partners, so the second person becomes the wheelbarrow. Now, as I've said, this is an intergenerational set of games, so prepare yourself for a very slow round when the children are carrying the grown-ups. These are the rules, and that's how you play, so no more complaining – get that wheelbarrow wobbling.

GAME 3: LEAPFROG
This is going to get especially interesting when there's a mixture of adults and children playing.

You will need:
Four or more players
A lawn or park to play in
A spring in your step

Classic partner style: this is the traditional way, in which one person crouches down, tucking in their head and curving their back. Then the second person takes a few fast steps before placing both hands upon on the middle of the first person's back, either side of the spine. They then spring themselves over their partner by opening their legs wide and pushing with their hands. Once they have leapt over, they then crouch down and the person who was leaped becomes the leaper. Make a start and a finish line and race all the way there, swapping over the leaper and the leaped every single time.

Relay: this slightly different variation can work with odd numbers in teams, but you will need to make a circle to race around (again, you can use jumpers as markers). Much like a relay race in the Olympics, each team spreads out around the track. However, instead of passing a baton between the players, you leapfrog your team-mate to tag them. They then run to the next player and leap them, setting them off, and so on. I would recommend doing enough rounds to make your way back to where you started, which means that everybody in the team will have jumped everybody else on the team.

Frog line: for this team version, you will need teams of ideally at least five people. Stand approximately two paces away from each other. Then the person at the back of the line leapfrogs over the backs of all of the other team members until they are at the front of the line. At this point they crouch down and the new person at the back begins the same process. The team that wins is the one that makes it over the finish line first, with their entire team completing all jumps.

Time trial: play this when there's not enough of you to have a proper leapfrog challenge. For this version, you will need some sort of timer such as a stopwatch on your phone, or even an old-fashioned egg timer. Form a line in front of each other and time how long it takes for each of you to leapfrog one another from start to finish. Adding in the time-trial element creates the momentum to push you to be slightly silly as you play.

LET THE REVOLUTION BEGIN!

The Real Play Revolution will begin when we stop believing that only certain things are possible and not possible, and when we start trying to make a difference anyway through the world of play – simply because it feels good. There's nothing that can make play more personal than creating an intergenerational community that is willing to muck in, spend time together – and have fun!

I hope you've enjoyed the last eight chapters of total twaddle, and that you feel you might be able to incorporate at least some of it into the play that you share with your kids or the groups you lead. While much of it might seem like explaining the obvious, sometimes I think we just need reminding that games are simple, and play is easy. All it really needs is some upbeat energy, fun ideas and that most important ingredient:

YOU

USEFUL RESOURCES

FURTHER READING

Fox, J. *Eyes on Stalks*, Methuen Drama, 2002.

Freire, P., *Pedagogy of the Oppressed*, Penguin, 2017.

Gerhardt, S., *Why Love Matters: How Affection Shapes a Baby's Brain*, Routledge, 2014.

Illich, I., *Deschooling Society*, Marion Boyars Publishers, 1995.

Robinson, K., *The Element: How Finding Your Passion Changes Everything*, Penguin, 2010.

Youdell, D. and Lindley, M.R., *Biosocial Education*, Routledge, 2018.

WEBSITES AND SOCIAL MEDIA

To find out more about The Flying Seagull Project and to join our flock, please visit our website: www.theflyingseagullproject.com

You can also follow our adventures on social media:

twitter.com/FlyingSeagullUK

www.facebook.com/flyingseagulls/

Comedic Commitment Contracts

Opposite is an example of a Comedic Commitment Contract. Feel free to cut out the template on page 173 and use it as the basis of your own contract, whether that is a Turkey Hat Grump Destroyer Contract, or a Red Nose Resolution Contract or any other type of Comedic Commitment Contract.

COMEDIC COMMITMENT CONTRACT
EXAMPLE

This contract, effective from Monday 2 September to Sunday 8 September, is a binding agreement between:

Amina Smith of 33 Park Road, New Town, England, AB1 2DE
and
Maya and Pete Smith (Mum and Dad) of 33 Park Road, New Town, England, AB1 2DE

The above-mentioned parties hereby agree to:
Have some fun by doing 30 seconds of clucking and waving our arms about like a chicken flapping its wings whenever one of us presses the red button!

The penalty for breach of contract is as follows:
Everyone thinking you are a spoilsport!

Exceptions to the terms of the contract are:
The red button is to be pressed no more than twice a day and only two times in public a week. Contract not in force when we are at Mum or Dad's office or at Granny's!

Signed by:

Amina Smith _____   Maya Smith + Pete Smith _____

Date: 31st May _____   Date: 31 May _____

Witnessed by: Joe Bloggs _____

Date: 31st May _____

COMEDIC COMMITMENT CONTRACT

This contract, effective from _____ to
_____, is a binding agreement between:

_____ of _____
and
_____ of _____

The above-mentioned parties hereby agree to:
_____
_____
_____
_____

The penalty for breach of contract is as follows:
_____
_____

Exceptions to the terms of the contract are:
_____
_____

Signed by:

_____   _____

Date: _____   Date: _____

Witnessed by: _____

Date: _____

INDEX

ACKNOWLEDGEMENTS

With grateful thanks for great ideas shared: rock star Andy, Harriet Shepherd, Joey Coconut, Hannelore and John Mowat.

For their continuous warmth, encouragement and support: Big Al Shaw, Heather, Ramiz Momeni, Sarah Wade and Lloyd Perrin.

For the hours of corrections and gold mining: Daniel Ashman.

For her brains and brawn: Professor Deborah Youdell. Jack Kelly, for his glorious scribbles; Sue Lascelles, for the amazing job of finding sense in the whirlwind and editing this book; Fiona, for her belief.

With thanks to Professor Deborah Youdell for permission to quote copyright material from "The Flying Seagull Project – Joining the Laugh-olution".

For launching the laughter: Naomi Briercliffe (AKA Norm), Matt Willis and Penny Mustill.

For their inspiration: Slava Polunin, Patch Adams, Jan King, Dr Hewitt, Anver the Eccentric.

Special thanks to all the children, families, and laughter-lovers that have been a part of this, and shared their love, light and laughter.

NOW PUT YOUR BOOK DOWN AND GO PLAY!

X

WATKINS

Sharing Wisdom Since 1893

The story of Watkins began in 1893, when scholar of esotericism John Watkins founded our bookshop, inspired by the lament of his friend and teacher Madame Blavatsky that there was nowhere in London to buy books on mysticism, occultism or metaphysics. That moment marked the birth of Watkins, soon to become the publisher of many of the leading lights of spiritual literature, including Carl Jung, Rudolf Steiner, Alice Bailey and Chögyam Trungpa.

Today, the passion at Watkins Publishing for vigorous questioning is still resolute. Our stimulating and groundbreaking list ranges from ancient traditions and complementary medicine to the latest ideas about personal development, holistic wellbeing and consciousness exploration. We remain at the cutting edge, committed to publishing books that change lives.

DISCOVER MORE AT:

www.watkinspublishing.com

Read our blog

Watch and listen to
our authors in action

Sign up to
our mailing list

We celebrate conscious, passionate, wise and happy living.
Be part of that community by visiting

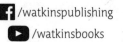